# ARISE AN

# ARISE & REAP

HODDER CHRISTIAN PAPERBACKS

ISABEL CHAPMAN

# ARISE AND REAP

## ISABEL CHAPMAN

*with Lucy Elphinstone*

**HODDER AND STOUGHTON**
LONDON SYDNEY AUCKLAND TORONTO

British Library Cataloguing in Publication Data

Chapman, Isabel
　Arise and reap.—(Hodder Christian paperback)
　1. Christian life
　I Title　　II. Elphinstone, Lucy
　284.4　　BV4501.2

ISBN 0 340 34157 2

*Hodder and Stoughton Editorial Office: 47 Bedford Square, London WC1B 3DP.*

To my mother, my family, the Children of Israel, my brethren in Christ Jesus, and all people everywhere:

> 'For God so loved the *world* that He gave His one and only Son, that whoever believes in Him shall not perish but have eternal life.'

(John 3: 16)

And this is my prayer: that your love may abound more and more in knowledge and depth of insight, *so that you may be able to discern what is best and may be pure and blameless until the day of Christ,* filled with the fruit of righteousness that comes through Jesus Christ – to the glory and praise of God.

Philippians 1: 9–11

# Acknowledgments

My meeting with Lucy Elphinstone was by divine appointment. Our Father had anointed her in a special way to minister through words on paper. I should like to express my gratitude to Lucy for her work and labour of love in presenting this book.

To those who have loved me, encouraged me, fed me and housed me, prayed for me and poured out their time and talents for me, I should like to give my warmest thanks: Peggy Noyce, Geoffrey and Tina Campbell-Black, Ron and Jean Taylor, Renée and Alex Joy, the Torbay Christian Fellowship, Upper Room Christian Fellowship, Great Yarmouth.

Scripture references are given in the New International Version except where indicated. In the Epilogue, the King James Version has been used, with the Living Bible for greater clarity. Wherever the Living Bible is given, the passage has been checked for correctness with other versions.

# Preface

Anyone less like a missionary I cannot imagine. Whether I really expected a prim and faded spinster with the definite air of a Latin mistress from a girls' boarding school, or a hearty Sunday School matron, equally at home pounding on the battered old piano or leading a bewildered group of natives in rounds of 'Bringing in the sheaves', all images were utterly dispelled as soon as Isabel Chapman stepped from the car. Nowhere could I see the Big Black Bag from which inevitably would be pulled an endless succession of photographs, slides, maps and coffee beans. Attractive, feminine, elegantly dressed, Isabel immediately struck me as a woman whose natural gifts would have guaranteed her every worldly success and esteem.

As we worked together on this book, I soon discovered that a sound Scottish matter-of-factness and a strong determination mingled richly with a lively sense of fun. But what impressed me most was the joy and openness with which she spoke about God. Isabel has an enthusiasm about the Lord which catches one up in a sense of His reality and love. Hearing her story, one soon understands why.

You have to be very sure of your God and of His guidance to sell all you own and go to a remote and primitive country without knowing a single person or what you are going to do there. Four months after becoming a Christian, Isabel was trudging through leech-infested rice paddies into the mountain regions of the headhunting tribes. In acute danger and often appalling conditions, she journeyed through areas where no other missionaries, nor any white man, had ever dared to venture. With just a handful of Filipino companions, Isabel shared the life and power of Jesus Christ, bringing salvation, healing and deliverance to hundreds of tribal people whose lives were bound by disease and idol worship.

It is an incredible story of faith and courage. And this dramatic ministry has continued ever since her return to England in 1981. Yet Isabel has been a Christian only three years. She has no theological training and no outstanding flair for public speaking. Despite (or perhaps because of) this, God has used her mightily in evangelistic and healing ministries, giving her also a specific prophetic message to preach concerning the imminent return of the Lord Jesus.

The key to such spiritual dynamism lies in a prophecy given over her in the United States in 1981. God said that He had chosen her because of her *obedience* and because of her *heart* in which His words would find a stable place. Profoundly aware of the futility and bondage from which the Lord had rescued her, Isabel put all she was and had at the Lord's disposal. He took her seriously. Throughout the past three years, her ministry has been characterised by this openness to His voice and a desire to do His will whatever the cost, trusting in His faithfulness to His words and not in her own ability.

When I asked Isabel what she felt to be her role in the scheme of God's purposes, she replied to bring salvation to the lost, to draw the Body of Christ together, to heal the sick, and to deliver the prophetic Word of God concerning the times in which we are living. The Lord told Isabel she was to be a 'repairer of the breach'. When that prophecy was given, Isabel did not understand what the Lord meant, but He has shown with increasing clarity that the breach is the period between the closing days of this world order and the establishment of the Lord's kingdom of peace on earth. Dying of typhoid fever, Isabel was miraculously healed, and given a revelation of the closing events of this world which will strengthen God's army and prepare it to stand firm in the days ahead.

It is not a revelation which can be easily or passively received, but her message is not intended to send people running to their burrows to hide. It is an unequivocal challenge to the Church, the Body of Christ, to step into the power and authority so abundantly available in these last days. God is pouring out His Spirit on all flesh so that His people can perform signs and wonders such as the world has never seen. It is an urgent call to non-Christians to recognise the living God before the darkness of the end overshadows the world.

But after the storm, the calm. In this generation, Isabel believes, the glory of the Lord will cover the earth. Her testimony bears witness to the truth of her message for it contains

> 'the signs of a true apostle performed
> in all patience, with signs and wonders
> and mighty works.'

*Lucy Elphinstone*

# Chapter One

The Filipino bus driver drove as if he had only a few hours left to live. With one hand on the steering wheel, the other on the horn, and a wild look in his eyes, he catapulted the battered old vehicle at breakneck speed along the narrow track. Every few minutes, a frenzied blast of the horn would send animals and people diving for safety as the bus careered past in clouds of dust. The hens in the cage jammed against my legs eventually recovered from their initial hysteria and collapsed in a dejected heap, occasionally giving a mournful cluck of despair. In the aisle and under the seats, bags of coconuts, boxes and crates of all shapes and sizes, full of fruit, vegetables and merchandise, rattled and slid as the bus lurched over potholes and swung dangerously round sharp bends. I looked for the reassuring sight of my suitcase, and saw it sinking forlornly under a sea of coconuts and oranges, like a wreck being covered by the tide, and I judged it impossible to wade to its rescue through the flood of luggage. In fact, most of my attention was absorbed simply in hanging on to my seat as the bus shook violently in its headlong rush, and I found myself wondering almost objectively at what point the whole contraption would finally disintegrate.

But soon it was the heat which became the dominant factor of that journey. It wound itself around my body like a hot, wet blanket, plastering my clothes to my skin, and draining all the energy and breath from my body. Just when I began to think that nothing would stop the lemming-like flight of the bus driver, he seemed to leap on the brakes with both feet and the bus shuddered to a breathless halt. As the dust settled, I saw that we were in a small town, humming with the confused activity of people buying, selling, begging, bargaining, shouting, laughing. Above the clamour, a voice called, 'Baloot! Baloot!' and two natives clambered on to the bus, one carrying a basket laden with corn on the cob, and the other bearing a box full of eggs. The man next to me bought an egg for two pesos and I watched fascinated as he cracked the egg on the back of the seat and began to peel off the shell. To my surprise the egg had been boiled, but as he plunged his teeth into the top with evident relish, my surprise turned to disgust, for inside was a half-formed chicken floating in black liquid. Lifting the rotten egg to his lips, the man poured the chicken and the liquid into his mouth, chewed meditatively and swallowed it with great satisfaction. I closed my eyes and tried to quell the feeling of nausea that heaved up from my stomach. 'Baloot', I later discovered, were eggs taken when nearly ready to hatch, boiled, and considered by the natives a particular delicacy.

After a few moments, I opened my eyes and saw someone else peel back the husk of a corn cob. Surely that was relatively harmless. I paid my peso and began to gnaw at the corn in the same way as the natives. All vestiges of taste had been boiled away but it relieved the hunger pains that had begun to claw at my stomach, and I was grateful.

I had been travelling for four days now, to and in a country where I knew not a soul and spoke not a single word of the language. My home, my job, my possessions were all gone, yet I still had no idea why the Lord had asked me to give up everything and go to the Philippine Islands, nor what work He had planned for me to do. As the bus spluttered into life again and headed for the mountains, I was suddenly assailed by the absurdity of the situation, and my weakness and inadequacy for any great task – even if one presented itself, which seemed a remote possibility just then.

It was January and the winter-whiteness of my skin, now pink and blotched with the heat, made me feel even more alien among the rich coffee colour of these people. Above the back of the next seat, a child's face appeared and two solemn black eyes stared in wonder at their first white woman. I smiled encouragingly but the eyes continued their amazed scrutiny, and I became acutely aware of the curious gazes of the other passengers. We seemed to belong to two different worlds, and for a moment I wondered helplessly how I could reach across the gulf of colour, language and culture. But the Father's faithfulness to me had never wavered, and as I lifted up my spirit to Him I saw a picture of the Lord Jesus on the Cross, His arms stretching out to east and west, embracing all men of every race in the greatness of His love. I realised then that there was no momentous task being set before me. The mighty act of sacrifice had been performed once and for all, bridging every gulf, destroying every barrier. The Lord's promise stood for eternity that complete provision had been made for all men to receive His everlasting life: 'And I, when I am lifted up from the earth, will draw all men to myself' (John 12. 32).

The burden slipped from my shoulders as I realised afresh that all the Lord was asking of me was obedience, to be open to His Word, and to trust in His ability. In every step of my short walk with Him, He had demonstrated His unfailing provision and love, and my heart flooded with joy once more as I reflected on the goodness which had brought me to this place.

## Chapter Two

I wasn't an obvious candidate for spiritual adventures – but then, Peter, Andrew, James and John hadn't shown much propensity for signs and wonders or public preaching during their years throwing nets into the Sea of Galilee. They hadn't taken a course in scripture knowledge and general miracles just in case the Messiah happened to walk along the seashore one day. But somehow God must have been working in their hearts, teaching them obedience and discipline, so that when the Master said, 'Follow Me', they were able to respond immediately. Again, the mighty works performed through them after Pentecost were not the result of the dynamism of their characters and their own wisdom, but the power of the Holy Spirit working in them, bearing the fruit of wholeness, order and peace in their own lives and in every situation. Yet they must have looked back and seen the Lord's hand upon them from the start, breaking, moulding, training, to form them into the channels of His grace and love. So it was with me – and with every one of His children.

There is nothing so fragile as the human heart, and none so vulnerable as a child's. No amount of reassurance could alleviate the sense of shock and the feeling of rejection and deception I experienced as an eight-year-old when I discovered that the man who had called himself my father was really my step-father, and that my parents had been divorced when I was two. In an undemonstrative family, it only needed a misunderstanding and an unfortunate remark to convince me that I was unwanted, and my pride made me furiously determined to relieve my step-father and my mother of my burdensome presence as soon as possible. It doesn't need two to make an argument. The rift between us was caused by my nurtured resentment, not by any harshness on my parents' part, but I was glad to leave home when my schooling finished at the age of fifteen, taking a job as a nanny just outside Edinburgh.

I had the useful ability to hide all this in a deep and well-protected corner of my soul, and my relationships with other people were warm and open. Like any young person, I chased excitement and happiness, but somehow in the heady pursuit my defences must have slipped and a disastrous relationship in my mid-twenties sent me stumbling blindly out of Scotland. Broken hearts are two a penny, but since we only have one the wound can be fatal, and my new life in England failed to heal the hurt. Pain subsides but the numbness that follows can be more crushing than any suffering, and the loneliness and futility of my existence in an alien environment crumbled away my sense of purpose. A calculated attempt at suicide inexplicably failed, so I determined to make no mistakes with the second. I swallowed enough tranquillisers to kill three people and sank into the oblivion I longed for.

For three days and three nights I lay unconscious until my eyes finally opened to behold the obstinate solidity of my bedroom ceiling. Incredulity and desolation washed over me. What horror was this that I couldn't even die? I dragged myself off the bed and staggered to the window of my seventh-storey flat. Far below, blobs of people swarmed meaninglessly along the grey pavements. I swayed over the edge of the window and suddenly my burning eyes focused on some organised movement at the foot of the building. A coffin was being carried out of the block of flats into a large black hearse. My confused brain reeled for a moment. Had I really died after all and my spirit was now watching this final journey of the corpse? But the pain in my head and the leaden weight of my limbs quickly persuaded me that I was still firmly in my mortal body. Despair wrung a cry from me. 'God, why won't you let me die?' Having lived most of my life without more than a passing reference to Him, I didn't really expect an answer, but at once I sensed a great presence in the room with me, and a distinct impression in my mind that the One who holds the keys of life and death had kept me in this world for a specific purpose, not as a sentence but as a gift, a commission. The person in the coffin had fulfilled his task but apparently my work still remained undone and the Lord's time for taking me had not yet come.

My lack of any feeling of self-worth made it hard to believe the idea that God had a special purpose for me, but at least it was painfully evident that trying to put an end to myself was a pointless task. As my physical strength returned over the next few days, I decided that if the world and I could not part company we had better make the most of the situation, and from somewhere the energy and a certain hope returned to enable me to move to another area and take a fresh job.

I determined to throw myself into my work, closing the door firmly on any idea of emotional involvements, and putting all my prospects of fulfilment in success and material prosperity. Finally I became a district agent for one of Britain's leading insurance companies and very soon the golden ladder of success began to materialise before me. As my salary steadily increased and my reputation and ability became more established, I began to feel that for the first time in my life I was gathering a little security to myself, and I devoured it hungrily.

By the age of thirty-three, I owned my own home, a comfortable bungalow which I had furnished lovingly and kept with fastidious care. The attention I gave my home stemmed from my desire to increase my sense of security and endow my life with some sort of meaning. God had not revealed any further plans for my life, but I knew deep down that I had closed my heart and mind to any demands He might make on me. My working relations with clients were excellent, with many developing into warm friendships for, on the surface, I was relaxed and outward-going. But I never let anyone come too close to the heavily barred area of my life where I could be hurt, and despite the fullness of my working hours, my private life remained empty. The gap still left by work, sleep, housework, eating and smoking, I tried to fill with hobbies, and I devoted much time and energy to collecting porcelain and breeding tropical fish.

But it was a hollow satisfaction. Ultimately, what worthwhile reward does one gain from cold, white china and bubble-blowing fish? Sometimes I would gaze bleakly back at their gaping stares and reflect that my own life was just as meaningless. I had to do something to stop these destructive thoughts and I began to have a drink each night when I returned from work, persuading myself that it was a good way to relax after a hard day of selling insurance. As the time passed, I found I was drinking more and more, and I began to look forward to the end of the day when I would be relaxing with my whisky in one hand and cigarette in the other. Drink, which had started off as a solace, a companion, became the dominant factor in my life. I became convinced that I would not be able to sleep without my 'nightcap' of a few strong whiskies. Eventually I admitted to myself that I was drinking too much but I was reassured by the fact that no one knew about it, as if the secrecy rendered it harmless. Besides, I never drank during working hours and what I did in the privacy of my own home was no one else's business. And so I retreated into this shell of self-deception.

# Chapter Three

Where can I go from your Spirit?
Where can I flee from your presence?
If I go up to the heavens, you are there;
if I make my bed in the depths, you are there.
If I rise on the wings of the dawn,
if I settle on the far side of the sea,
even there your hand will guide me,
your right hand will hold me fast.
If I say, 'Surely the darkness will hide me
and the light become night around me,'
even the darkness will not be dark to you;
the night will shine like the day,
for darkness is as light to you (Ps. 139: 7–12).

The Lord has a long arm – and infinite love. No pit is too
deep or dark for Him to be able to reach down to the one
imprisoned there. Nor is He ever too far to be able to hear the
unspoken cry of the heart. I had long ago written myself off
as not worth God's time or attention, but His love works
according to a different scale from ours, not reason but
grace. Where would any of us be if retribution rather than
mercy governed God's actions towards us? Just at the point
where I least deserved it, His grace abounded to me and the
course of my life was dramatically changed.

It seemed a harmless enough day. Perhaps its very
mundanity lowered my defences so that when one of my
clients gently yet earnestly asked me if I would accompany
her to a Full Gospel Businessmen's dinner, I found myself
accepting before I had time to weigh up the implications.
The Full Gospel Businessmen's Fellowship, Mrs Graham
explained, was an organisation designed to convey the whole

power of the Christian gospel to people in every sort of trade and profession, revealing Christianity not as a matter of church attendance but acceptance of the Lordship of Jesus Christ and the in-dwelling of His Holy Spirit. None of this meant much to me. All I gathered was that it was religious and there was nothing I less wanted to get involved with. Yet it was kind of her to ask me, and to refuse later would have seemed so rude.

Nevertheless, as the day drew nearer, the whole idea became more absurd and I began to rack my brains for some convincing excuse. I felt sure I should look and feel so out of place, especially if there was a lot of praying and holy talk going on, and I kept imagining how infinitely more comfortable my own fireside would be with a soothing whisky in my hand. By five o'clock on the day of the dinner, I had failed to come up with a plausible excuse, so with a heavy heart I bathed and dressed. Being ready early, I was just reaching for a drink to pass the time and fortify myself, when the words 'gospel dinner' jumped into my mind. I could picture the disapproving looks if I turned up at a religious meeting reeking of whisky. Not wanting to embarrass my friend, I quickly drove to the local hotel and swallowed a double vodka which I thought no one would be able to smell. Then with a bright smile I picked up Mrs Graham and drove to the hotel where the dinner was being held.

The moment I entered the room, my stomach seemed to tie itself in a knot, and my tongue seemed to stick to the roof of my mouth. All around me were warmth and friendliness, yet I was conscious only of my sense of guilt and inferiority as I remembered that accusing glass of vodka. I hardly dared open my mouth in case anyone guessed I had been drinking.

Most of what was said by the speakers about their experiences of coming to know Jesus went over my head, I felt so engulfed by my sense of shame and inadequacy but, towards the end of the meeting, the main speaker asked people to come forward and give their lives to Jesus. The words acted like a trigger. Suddenly I saw myself as a child of seven, going to a gospel meeting with my cousin and hearing

22

of the love that Jesus had for me. I remembered giving my heart to Him and, like a forgotten dream, the memory of how happy I had felt came flooding back. I saw a little child singing a gospel chorus with bright, earnest eyes, and my heart ached to know the joy of belonging to Jesus once more, the joy which had been crushed by my step-father's decision that 'all that hallelujah stuff' was not good for a child of that age. I had grown up and grown away from my Jesus, but now I seemed to see Him again, holding out His hand and I longed to reach out and touch Him once more.

The speaker's voice broke upon my dream, 'Come forward and give your life to Jesus.' I wanted to move but my feet were rooted to the spot, and it was only the gentle encouragement of a young woman sitting near me which had me stumbling blindly to the front of the room where the speaker laid his hands on me and began to speak in a language I didn't understand.

No façade or barrier can withstand the piercing touch of the Lord's love when He sets His hand upon a person. The walls of self-sufficiency and pride crumbled, the prison of my insecurity and rejection was broken down, and I stood before my Father as I really was, a helpless child in desperate need of forgiveness, healing and love.

It is good that wisdom and gentleness rule all His dealings with us. My sin and worthlessness lay starkly before me, but during that meeting I also saw the purity of the Son and I knew that His death on the Cross paid the penalty for my sin and made that wholeness available to me. His joy, peace, health and power could be my own experience if I repented of my sins and surrendered my whole being to Him.

That evening I asked Jesus to forgive me of my sins, to come into my life and mould me into the person He wanted me to be. It was as if the Lord took away my heart of stone and gave me a heart of flesh, for I not only knew His forgiveness but I felt the warmth of His love. For the first time, I knew that I was of worth to someone, that I was precious to my Father, not because of or even in spite of who I was or what I had done, but simply because I was His child, bought by the blood of Jesus and sharing in His character and inheritance.

The woman sitting beside me invited me to go to her church the following Sunday and I agreed with enthusiasm, amazed at the transformation in my heart. I felt as if I had only just begun to live and I was eager to take my first steps.

## Chapter Four

I had never noticed before the awful, stale smell of cigarette smoke in my home, but suddenly the acrid fumes nearly knocked me on my back when I returned home that night. As the week passed, I began to hate the filthy habit of smoking, and I saw the drinking for what it was, not as a harmless solace but a futile and destructive means of escapism. I decided that when the whisky I had in the house was finished, I would not buy any more. After that I resolved I would give up smoking. It was easy coming to that decision; it seemed so obvious, so easy, merely a question of the will. I had no idea that putting it into practice would prove so different.

The church I attended the following Sunday was the complete opposite of the stereotype I had in mind, and the people I met equally contradicted my expectations. I had never encountered people so full of joy and love. I was made to feel very welcome and it seemed as though I had become part of a new family. I found that my brothers and sisters were united in a love and enthusiasm for the Father that overflowed in songs and prayers of praise, and as the service moved into worship I began to glimpse the beauty and majesty of God.

At one point something strange yet wonderful happened. I didn't understand it, but it touched something deep within me, and I knew that it was coming from the very courts of heaven. During some singing, a clear bell-like voice sounded above the others, and words in a strange language yet full of an unearthly beauty rang through the church. Gradually other voices mingled in perfect harmony, and soon it seemed as if the whole congregation was caught up in the heavenly chorus. I imagined it was like the singing of angels and when I asked someone at the end of the service I discovered it was indeed a heavenly language, the gift of tongues, inspired by the Holy Spirit, which only God understands. It was a glorious revelation to learn that we could come into this intimate relationship with the Godhead and I looked forward to experiencing more of the power of God in my life.

By the following evening all the alcohol in the house was finished and I was determined that this was the end. A subtle change had occurred within me and in my mind I no longer had any desire to drink or smoke. I saw no attraction in them for I had come to view them as an abuse both to my body and to the Holy Spirit dwelling within that temple. I confidently looked forward to freedom from their slavery, but immediately discovered I was bound by another law which overruled my will. A battle seemed to be raging inside me. One half of me wanted to give up the drink but the other half craved for it, and by nine o'clock that night my body was screaming out for a drink. I paced up and down the floor, clenching my fists, my forehead beaded with perspiration, and every so often a more insidious voice would rise above the clamour, whispering that I needed a drink to relax after such a hard day's work, insisting that a small glass of whisky would be the only thing to send me to sleep that night. Suddenly something snapped inside me and I found myself fumbling feverishly at the car door and driving violently to the off-licence for the bottle that would satisfy the terrible craving.

It was the start of a dependence far worse than anything I had known before. Every morning I would say that the coming evening would see the last drop but each time the battle would defeat me and I seemed to drink more and more to forget the feeling of guilt and failure. For three weeks I endured this torment, and although I was deeply worried by the half bottle of whisky I was consuming each night, my mind seemed unable to crush the insatiable craving.

I had never been one to share my problems but desperation forced me to reveal the situation to one of the young women I had met at church. I was amazed to hear that she had once been a drug addict and unable to kick the habit, but Jesus had delivered her from the bondage which had dominated her life. I did not really understand what she meant by deliverance but I was ready to grasp at any hope so I arranged to meet her at the church the following Wednesday before the meeting for prayer and Bible ministry.

I do not know how I reached the church, for an invisible army seemed to be buffeting my body and tearing me apart inside. Nevertheless, somehow my legs carried me there, and as soon as I entered the building I began to cry uncontrollably. Even as a child I had rarely cried and in latter years had shunned any demonstration of strong emotion, but now I could not stop myself, yet I could not understand why. To my embarrassment, a number of people had gathered round about me and I found myself telling one of the elders that I had a drinking problem. I shall never forget the words he spoke to me.

'Do you really *want* to give up drinking?' he asked, his keen eyes searching my face.

'Yes, with all my heart, soul and body,' I replied.

The second these words left my mouth, the power of God came down upon me. I felt the feeling drain out of my body, and I fell face down on the floor. Part of me wanted to get up and run away, but some unseen power, not human hands, was pinning me to the ground and I could not move. What happened next was remarkable. My spirit left my body and I felt as if I was suspended somewhere near the ceiling of the church. I could see my body lying on the floor with a knot of people kneeling beside it. As they began to pray in tongues, something in my body began to scream, and my legs and arms started to kick and thrash wildly. The scream was a tortured, inhuman sound wrung from the depths of my being. Finally the screaming subsided, and I found that I was back in my body again. The first thing I realised was that an enormous weight had been lifted from me. Then I felt the throbbing rawness of my throat. It had been a terrifying experience and I could not really understand what had happened except that I knew I had been set free that night. Hitherto I had only believed in evil as an abstract force, but now I knew the reality of the Devil and I saw that God had taken my spirit out of my body, and delivered me from the evil spirits which had been controlling and dominating my life.

A little while later, I climbed into bed, exhausted and rather frightened. Sleep seemed impossible: as I lay there the shadows in the room suddenly solidified into a fearful black shape which moved towards me, threatening to engulf me. Terrified, I clutched my Bible to my chest and said again and again, 'By the blood of Jesus, keep away from me. By the blood of Jesus, keep away from me.'

Out of the darkness, a great red drop of blood fell on the black spirit and in a moment it shrivelled up and disappeared. Peace, peace filled the room and I felt a depth of security and trust I had not known before. I knew that never again would I be tempted by drink, but more importantly I had won my first battle over the Devil by faith in the blood of Jesus. It was a lesson which established the foundation of my walk with Him from that moment on. Not only did I discover the power and authority that is ours in the name of Jesus, but I recognised for myself from this early stage that our fight is not against 'flesh and blood, but against persons without bodies – the evil rulers of the unseen world, those mighty satanic beings and great evil princes of darkness who rule this world; and against huge numbers of wicked spirits in the spirit world' (Eph. 6: 12, LB).

I was glad to know from the beginning that full provision is made not only for our protection, but also for our *victory* over every attack, and since then I have always tackled problems at their spiritual root rather than simply in their physical manifestation.

## Chapter Five

There was now no barrier to the channel of the Lord's love and healing. Years of resentment and self-condemnation were washed away, and in place of that root of insecurity was planted the assurance of His unfailing care and commitment. My Father loved me! Not only that, but He valued me as a precious jewel, a crown of beauty and a royal diadem in His hand. He had set such store on me that He had delivered me from the powers of darkness and given meaning and purpose to my life. His Holy Spirit began to work within me, and my whole outlook gradually changed, altering my sense of values and overwhelming my heart with a desire to know and love Him more.

Soon afterwards I was baptised in water to demonstrate before men and angels that my old life was behind me and that from then on I was going to lead my life according to His will and Word. I rose from the water knowing that my past was buried for ever with Christ Jesus and that I was free to enjoy the glorious newness of abundant life in Him. No guilt or regret could now obstruct the wonderful personal relationship I had discovered with my Lord and Saviour, for I knew that 'There is therefore no condemnation for those who are in Christ Jesus. For the law of the Spirit of life in Christ Jesus has set me free from the law of sin and death' (Rom. 8: 1–2). Nothing could separate me from His love.

Luke recounts the story of Simon the Pharisee who once invited Jesus to eat in his house and then was scandalised when a woman with a dubious reputation was allowed to kneel, weeping, at His feet, anointing them with ointment from an alabaster flask and wiping them with her hair. Jesus, after asking Simon the question about the creditor with two debtors, says to him, 'Her sins, which are many, are forgiven,

29

for she loved much; but he who is forgiven little, loves little' (Luke 7: 47). My awareness of how much He had forgiven rebounded in love and thanksgiving to the Lord. Each new day seemed a gift from my Father, dawning full of hope and significance, and I longed to express my love for Him better.

It was late October, only a few weeks since I had given my life to the Lord, and His touch was mellowing the whole world into the rich warm shades of autumn. One morning, when I was driving to work, the day seemed aflame with the glow of gold and russet in the trees and hedgerows. Above me a cloudless sky throbbed a deep clear blue and the sunlight streamed through the leaves, dappling the road with pools of brightness. My heart swelled with joy and as my spirit lifted in praise I took my hands off the steering wheel and threw them in the air. 'Jesus, I love you, and I give myself to you one hundred per cent, all that I am and all that I have. Just use me for your glory.'

A sense of expectancy and excitement stayed with me all that day, and my spirit seemed as if it would burst as I searched for words to tell of my love and gratitude to Him. Then I remembered the heavenly language by which the Holy Spirit Himself can pray through us, so the following morning I prayed, as best I could,

Thank you, Lord Jesus, for dying for me. I believe that you are God's Son and that I am His child too. I want to be a good Christian and follow you all the days of my life. Lord Jesus, I should like to be able to pray in the spirit directly to you. Please fill me completely with your Holy Spirit and give me the gift of tongues.

No sooner had I spoken, than strange and beautiful words began to tumble from my lips. I did not understand with my mind what I prayed but I knew that my spirit was caught up with His, pouring out, unhindered, my praise and adoration. It was a precious gift and day by day I learnt to pray and worship more freely in my new heavenly language.

A few days later, I was sitting reading my Bible one afternoon when the Lord spoke to my heart with a still, small voice. Gently, yet distinctly, these words were impressed upon me, 'Isabel, I want more from you.' Deeply surprised, I sat there and thought about it until I was convinced that I had been mistaken. In a flash, the Lord brought every event of my life before me in a vision and showed me how in each one His hand had always been upon me. My life was not my own but His from the very beginning. It was only afterwards that I learnt that 'Isabel' was from a Hebrew word meaning 'consecrated to God'.

My imagination immediately began to fly in all directions. I applied my mind and reason to all sorts of possibilities, but nothing seemed to bring the Lord's confirmation. So I came to learn, 'A man's mind plans his way, but the Lord directs his steps' (Prov. 16: 9).

The Lord had His own time and way of letting me know what His plan was for me. One Sunday evening, a visiting preacher came to the church and, under his anointed speaking, the Holy Spirit began to move powerfully in people's lives. The only thing I can remember of that sermon are the words, 'The harvest is plentiful but the workers are few.' As I heard these words, my heart inexplicably began to beat twice as fast as normal and was thumping so hard that I could hear it throbbing in my head. Other members of the church were going forward for ministry, and the next moment I found myself walking down the aisle and kneeling in front of the altar. What happened then is difficult to describe. I was kneeling on the floor, my arms raised in the air, faintly aware of praying in tongues, when the Spirit of the Lord seemed to catch me up and for a moment oblivion blocked out all sensation and consciousness and I was immersed in the mighty presence of God. When I came back to myself, I astounded myself, for the first words that came out of my mouth were, 'I am going to the Philippine Islands.' No thought or reasoning of my own had produced that declaration. I had no idea where on the map the Philippines were!

For days afterwards the words pounded through my brain, 'I'm going to the Philippines, I'm going to the Philippines,' but the idea was so ludicrous that I had no peace of mind. My heart had sunk when I had finally located them on the map, far off in the South China Sea, and I could not imagine what God could want with an insurance saleswoman in that remote spot. Surely the only reason God called a person to far-off lands was to be a missionary. But I had no academic or medical qualification to equip me for missionary work and, besides, I was very comfortable in the niche I had established for myself in East Anglia.

Finally I could stand it no longer. Prowling restlessly up and down the sitting-room floor, I halted abruptly and demanded, 'Lord, how *can* I go to the Philippines? What about my work – and what about my home?' Quietly, authoritatively, His words impressed themselves upon me with utter certainty, 'Sell what you own and give up your work.' I was stunned. But there was no escaping the reality and firmness of that command.

I waited until the weekly Bible study at the church, and after the meeting I approached the pastor and told him that I believed God was calling me to the Philippines. He was kind but firm. I was just a baby Christian and if I really wanted to be a missionary I should have to spend at least six months in Bible college.

'You can't just take off and go on to the mission field with no experience or Bible training,' he insisted gently. 'I'm sorry, Isabel, but I have to tell you that you can't go. The Lord doesn't take novices on the mission field.'

I left the church that evening in turmoil. I was sure that God had spoken to me, but maybe the pastor was right. What good could I do by going out there? My Bible knowledge was indeed poor, and I knew I should have difficulty teaching a Sunday School class, let alone go on the mission field. I knew the pastor had my best interests at heart and I could not go against the counsel of his wisdom and experience. I decided that perhaps the best policy was just to forget the whole thing.

But I felt torn in two directions, and at last I took the situation to the Lord in prayer.

'My father in heaven, I come to You in the name of Jesus. Please help me. I feel sure that You spoke to me and told me to sell what I own, give up my job and go to the Philippines.

Lord, You heard the conversation between my pastor and me. I don't want to go against him, but I want to carry out Your will. Please show me what I should do.'

The Lord's answer was swift and sure. That still voice I had grown to recognise spoke clearly to my heart. 'Can you stand in obedience to Me and do what I want you to do though people speak against you?'

'Yes, Lord,' was my certain reply. Now I had no doubts. Whatever the opposition, I would go ahead and do what I knew God wanted of me. My mind was made up and I was determined to listen to no one except the Holy Spirit. His voice is not always the easiest or most comfortable to hear, but there is peace only in the will of God, however reasonable and well-meaning human advice may be.

There is only one way to respond to a command from the Lord. Immediately. I rang the estate agents and asked them to come and view my property, explaining that I was going abroad and wanted a quick sale. The next step was my letter of resignation. It was a difficult letter to write for I wanted to convey that I enjoyed my work and that my reasons for leaving were not provoked by the company, nor, in fact, had anything to do with the work itself. I made an appointment with the district manager and spent the next few days nervously trying to picture the conversation that would take place. It was hard to imagine that his response to my explanation of missionary work would be one of credibility, let alone enthusiasm.

Eventually I presented myself outside his door with a sinking heart. A few moments later, I was sitting opposite his huge desk, feeling rather like a schoolchild presenting its lines to the headmaster. My rehearsed speech seemed to dissolve into the air under his scrutinising gaze. Haltingly, I began in a way that could hardly have inspired confidence.

'I don't quite know how to tell you this but I might as well just say it and get it over with. I made this appointment today to tell you that I want to hand in my resignation.'

He blinked in surprise, but said nothing, so I ploughed on, trying to make my voice sound calm and positive. 'I enjoy my work and get on very well with my clients – in fact, I shall be sorry to say goodbye to many of them – so my leaving has nothing at all to do with the company, the work or the people I deal with.' Now I took a deep breath and looked him straight in the eye. 'God has called me to go to the Philippine Islands to do missionary work.'

It certainly provoked a response. Mr Lawn swallowed hard twice, and then exploded, 'God has WHAT?!' he demanded, the look of total unbelief on his face making me squirm in my seat. 'I wasn't aware you were religious. When did this happen?'

I explained that I had always believed in God but now I had a real relationship with the Lord Jesus. I tried to describe to him my experience in church and how the Lord had carried me out in the spirit, but perhaps that was a mistake for now his look of incredulity turned to one of deep concern and pity.

'I won't accept your resignation at this point, Isabel,' he told me, firmly. 'I'm sure you must have been talking to some of these religious cranks on your agency. You go away and think about it, and when you're feeling better, come back and see me in a few days. I'm sure you will have got over all this by then.'

The interview was at an end. He stood up, dismissively, and I walked miserably to the door, feeling utterly confused, still clutching my letter of resignation. Had I really just got carried away and would all this pass in a couple of days? Had I become a little unbalanced? I reached out to my Heavenly Father, and immediately the assurance of His leading flooded into my heart and His challenge to my obedience and courage rang again in my ears. No, I will not listen to these thoughts and doubts, I told myself resolutely. I know that God has called me.

I went about my work in the normal way for the next three days, then I rang the manager's office and made another appointment. He ushered me in and I sat down, the letter of resignation feeling heavy as lead. He looked at it regretfully.

'So you haven't had a change of heart?' I shook my head firmly, and he continued, 'I've made some enquiries about your situation. I rang a minister who is a friend of mine and he explained that sometimes people do get too enthusiastic and carried away when they first get involved in religion but normally, after a short time, they settle down.'

'I haven't been carried away,' I replied, steadily. 'I know that God wants me to give up my job, sell what I own and go abroad.'

'How do you know that?'

'I just know that I know,' I found myself saying, which sounded ridiculous even to me, but I felt powerless to explain the reason for my certainty. Mr Lawn struggled with his patience and then, like a teacher trying to communicate with a backward child, he leant forward and asked in a tone of studied reasonableness, 'What are you going to do when you get there?'

'I don't know,' I replied. 'All I know is God wants me to go.'

'Have you any kind of missionary training?'

'No.'

'What about the language? Will you able to communicate with these people?'

'I can only speak English.'

A note of exasperation began to creep into his measured questions. 'Have you had any medical training?'

'Never,' I replied. This was hopeless. All I could do was sit there, uncomfortable and embarrassed, feeling about two inches tall in the eyes of this rational and experienced businessman.

'I don't want to go on at you, Isabel, but it does sound to me as if the whole thing is just a bit too absurd.' If he found that hard to believe, he was flabbergasted by my next words.

'I shall lay hands on the sick and they will be healed in the name of Jesus Christ!' I was as astonished as he was. I had had no intention of saying such a thing, nor had I ever thought it, but the words were out of my mouth before I could stop them. That did it. He looked at me, then at my hands, and finally reached out to take my letter of resignation.

'Perhaps you should take a long holiday, Isabel,' he suggested kindly but without much conviction. 'And maybe a psychiatrist could help . . .' His voice trailed off uncertainly as he showed me to the door.

Outside I wondered again if I could possibly be in my right mind. People just do not give up a good job, sell what they own and go off to a strange country where they do not know anyone, I reasoned, and in my confusion I turned once more to the Lord.

'Lord Jesus, please help me to fulfil your plan in my life. I am weak but I know I can do all things through your strength.'

It was just six weeks since I had gone to that Full Gospel dinner.

## Chapter Six

I had always spent my money as I earned it. There was not even enough money in the bank to pay my fare abroad. But this was no obstacle to Him who created the whole universe simply by His Word of power. I made an appointment with the bank manager, and before I left home I prayed, 'My Father in heaven, if this is your will, please touch the manager's heart so that he will lend me the money I shall need. I ask this in the name of Jesus.'

'How can I help you, Miss Chapman?' asked the stern-faced man behind the huge black desk. I began to explain that I had just handed in my resignation at work and was planning to go abroad to do missionary work, but had no funds or means of supporting myself. My bungalow was up for sale and in the meantime could he lend me some money to tide me over until the sale of the property. He did not seem unduly surprised and asked casually, 'What missionary organisation are you joining?'

This was the crunch. Prepared for the look of amazement, then pity and a nervous glance at the door, I nevertheless tried to answer with equal coolness, 'I'm going completely on my own and shall be getting my instructions directly from God.'

The great man did not flinch. It probably takes a lot to shock a bank manager. He sat there and stared at me penetratingly for what seemed like an age and I just looked steadily back at him.

'How much money do you want?' he asked at last, his eyes maintaining their stern scrutiny.

'Three thousand pounds will be fine,' I replied lightly, as if it were sixpence. He rose from the desk abruptly but instead of a scandalised protest, he merely said matter of factly, 'I'll go and get the necessary papers for your signature.'

Within a few minutes, the documents were signed and I walked out of the bank with three thousand pounds at my disposal. I could hardly believe it had been so easy. All the way home the car rang with my praise and thanks to God for this tremendous assurance of His leading and provision, deeply aware that I was walking in the path prepared by Him.

I was now working my notice and it seemed only right that I should tell all my clients that I was leaving. Many seemed to think it a brave thing to do and hoped everything would go well for me; others were perhaps more honest and said plainly that I was crazy to give up a good job and a nice home for vague missionary work in a foreign country.

The office was buzzing with talk about me but the Lord's confidence and peace meant that their jokes and even outright laughter and scorn did not hurt or offend me. As I walked into the office one day, someone said, 'This is the person you want to see about that boil. She reckons she can lay hands on you and you will be healed!'

Amidst the laughter another voice quipped, 'She can lay hands on me any time she wants but she has to let me lay hands on her in return!'

I closed the door quietly on their hoots of derision, heavy at heart for their ignorance and superficiality. 'Father, forgive them,' I prayed, 'for they don't know what they are saying.'

The Lord had already shown me He was a practical God and concerned with even the smallest detail of our life. His commitment to His Word meant that He not only told me to sell all I possessed, but He set about providing a way. As I called on my clients and said my last farewells, it often came out in conversation that I should be selling all my furniture, carpets and procelain, and one by one people began to show an interest in different items. One customer discovered that my three-piece suite was exactly what she was looking for and bought it on the spot. Another couple needed new bedroom furniture and someone else wanted the washing machine. It was like the first half hour of a village fete. My belongings were scooped up in rapid succession, the cooker, tumble-dryer, dining chairs, desk... Nothing remained except the refrigerator, a beautiful Indian carpet, the tropical fish and the collection of porcelain displayed in its elegant cabinet. I arranged to exhibit the porcelain, some pieces of which were collector's items and limited editions, but one couple fell in love with the whole display and I found myself selling the lot in one package. The delighted couple were incredulous.

'How could you just give up items of such beauty like this?' they demanded. But I had absolutely no regrets. They were only worldly possessions and did not mean anything to me any more. I took my jewellery to a second-hand shop and sold it all, no longer feeling that I needed to impress by wearing expensive necklaces and rings. For I knew that I had discovered a pearl of great price and no money could buy the preciousness of the Spirit of the living God within me.

My ticket was bought and I was due to fly in mid-January. I intended to go home to Scotland for Christmas as this would give me a chance to tell my mother personally what I was planning to do, rather than trying to explain it all by phone or letter. By this time the news had spread round the church and community in Norwich that I was going ahead with the idea of going abroad, against the advice of pastor, employer and friends, and everyone was of the same opinion – that I was making a great mistake. People tried reason, persuasion, even admonition, but although their disapproval or concern saddened me as I would have welcomed their support, I knew that I had to be obedient to the Lord before everything and I gently refused their well-meaning advice.

One Sunday evening, I was asked by someone in the church whereabouts in the Philippines I would be going. I could only answer that I did not know yet, so at home I took the question to the Lord in prayer.

'It will be revealed to you when you go home to Scotland,' came the Lord's Word to my heart, and I rejoiced in the peace which that promise brought.

39

I flew from Norwich to Aberdeen, then hired a car for the rest of the journey to my mother's house. My step-father had died a few years before and she now lived alone. I drove along, pondering deeply how I could explain to my mother my future plans. For about thirty minutes I had been following a long lorry and at last we came to a straight piece of road that would allow me to overtake. Far down the road, a white car was approaching but I knew there was plenty of time to get past, so I put my foot down on the accelerator and began to overtake. I was half-way past the lorry when the driver suddenly started to indicate and pull out towards me. My immediate reaction was to brake but as I pumped the brakes I realised I had been travelling too fast to get back. The lorry was bearing down on me from the left, a stone wall loomed on my right, and the white car in front seemed almost upon me. In my mind's eye, I saw the impact of the crash. Closing my eyes, I gripped the steering wheel and braced myself for the head-on collision. But none came. Amazed, I opened my eyes and found myself back behind the lorry. I knew that I had not driven the car into this position and I could not see how the terrible crash had been avoided except that the mighty hand of God had intervened. My spirit sang at the abundance of the Lord's grace which had saved my life and that of the driver in the white car. I travelled on in safety to my mother's home.

The next few days were spent with my family, sharing with them the miracle that had happened in my life and God's sure call to go to the Philippine Islands. To some extent words were superfluous, for the Lord had done such a work of healing in my heart of the old hurts and resentments that I overflowed with a new love for my dear mother which erased all the bitter memories. She could see that I was a different person but she kept her feelings to herself until, at exactly fifteen minutes to midnight on Christmas Eve, she asked the Lord Jesus to forgive her of her sins and come into her life. High above, the angels of heaven welcomed a new baby into the kingdom.

The following day, I visited the home of one of my cousins, and as I sat and talked about my planned trip abroad, she told me of a Filipino group which had called at their church some years ago and had made a record. She gave me the address of the group on the album and I put it in my purse. Soon afterwards, another cousin mentioned the same group and gave me a photograph of a Filipino woman who was one of the singers on the record. Written on the back of the snapshot was the name, Mercy. I put the photograph with the address in my purse but soon forgot about them, thankful to my thoughtful cousins but holding out little hope that the information would be of any use. It seemed a remote possibility indeed that our paths would cross in the vast expanse of that remote country.

My four days passed all too swiftly and I had to return to Norwich to work my last week's notice. As I prepared to leave on the final morning, my mother looked troubled and at the door her hand grasped my arm tightly.

'Isabel dear – are you sure you're doing the right thing?' I was glad of the new-found tenderness between us that enabled me to reassure her that she need not worry because Jesus would take care of me and I knew that I was doing His will. One last hug, and the door closed behind me. I turned my face to the south.

## Chapter Seven

My last week's notice was worked and only final arrangements remained. The little bungalow was empty except for the refrigerator, the Indian carpet and the tropical fish which swam worriedly round their tank, mouthing great 'Oos' of astonishment. As I lay on my borrowed camp bed one night, I thought about the beautiful carpet, which had attracted many offers, but for some reason I had always turned them down. 'I'll put it into store,' I decided with relief. 'One day I might come back and then it will be waiting for me.' But I knew in my heart that the Lord had told me to sell *all* I owned. In trying to keep the carpet, I was holding on to my last vestiges of security and not surrendering myself totally to God. In the watches of the night, I let go completely and asked the Lord what He wanted to do with the carpet. Immediately I saw a vision of a young pregnant girl walking with bare feet on naked floor boards, and the Lord said, 'Give her the carpet.'

I knew who the girl was. She and her husband had recently moved to the area and it was obvious they were extremely poor for the husband was unemployed and could not afford to pay their insurance premiums. I felt great peace as I loosed my last foothold, and I was glad at the comfort and happiness the couple would soon know.

The carpet was large and heavy, so next day I hired a removal van to transport it to their house. I felt no misgivings as the men rolled it up and threw it casually into the back of the van. When we arrived there, however, there was no reply to our knock, and as I did not want the trouble of taking the carpet a second time, we left it against the front door. The following day I asked a friend of mine to go and check that the young couple had found the carpet when they returned home. To my utter astonishment, I found that the carpet was at the police station! Unknown to me, the husband had a friend who worked in a carpet factory. The friend was not entirely honest and had promised the young couple that he would 'acquire' a carpet for them. When they found the rare and valuable carpet on their doorstep, they were horrified, feeling sure that the police would soon trace the theft of something so costly and, reluctantly, they had reported the strange appearance of presumably stolen property.

I rang the police station and explained the carpet's unusual history, asking them to return it to the couple's house. To my relief, the officer in charge reacted with some amusement. 'I wish I'd known you,' he joked, 'then you might have left it on my doorstep.' But I was praising God for the bizarre incident for I saw that He had used the carpet not only to meet this young couple's need but also to prevent their friend from stealing and them from receiving stolen property. The Lord certainly does hold the world in the palm of His hand. A way seemed open to tell them of His goodness, so I went round and found the young wife absolutely thrilled with the carpet but a little concerned that her husband might sell such an expensive commodity and buy a cheaper one, seeming ungrateful for the gift.

'It's not my gift but God's,' I explained to her astonishment, and went on to tell her that it was not my idea to give them the carpet but that God had told me to do so in a vision.

'Besides,' I laughed, 'I shall be thousands of miles away in a few weeks' time, doing missionary work, so I won't know *what* happens to the carpet!' There was a moment's pause, and then she turned to me shyly, 'If he does sell the carpet, your Lord will tell you, won't He?' I smiled, rejoicing that His love was already touching her life with the under-standing of His reality and care. Maybe the Lord was moving into more than just the emptiness of their house!

My poor distracted fish had found a home at last, and as I was preparing for the tank to be removed one morning, it suddenly dawned on me that I had been to Scotland and returned home again, but still had no idea where in the Philippines the Lord wanted me to go. I turned to Him at once and raised up my perplexity. Immediately I felt I should fetch my handbag and, opening my purse, I saw the utterly forgotten address and photograph my cousins had given me. I was puzzled and rather unbelieving, for I couldn't see what use I could be to a singing group.

'If this is really where You want me to go, Lord,' I found myself saying, 'then I want to be sure. Please let someone in Norwich know the girl's name.'

The following Sunday after church, I was talking to one of the ladies, who expressed an interest in buying my refrigerator. A few days later, she and her husband came round to see it and agreed a price. Then, over a cup of coffee, she said carefully, 'I can hardly believe you're really giving up all you have in this way. Are you absolutely sure you are doing the right thing?' In response to my patient assurance, she continued philosophically, 'Well, time will tell.' Then she brightened, 'If it's not of God, you can always come back and start all over again.'

I smiled inwardly for I was learning that it was no good trusting God if one prepared security plans and contingency schemes. Faith could only work when fear, doubt and all negative thinking were banished.

'Whereabouts in the Philippines are you going, Isabel?' was her next question. In reply, I showed her the address and photograph, explaining that this was all I had. In an instant she had grasped the photograph and was exclaiming excitedly, 'But I know this girl! Her name is Mercy. She and her group stayed with our pastor some years ago when they were doing a tour of this country.'

What little trust we have when we are dumbfounded by the answer to our prayers. I sat there, speechless for a moment, drinking in God's goodness in this marvellous confirmation, then I threw my arms in the air and cried, 'Praise the Lord!' Now I knew exactly where He wanted me to go. My dependence remained on Him, though, for I was due to fly the following Monday and there was no time to write and advise anyone of my arrival. His peace was my security and confidence.

Last-minute arrangements had to be made. I put the sale of my property into the hands of my solicitor and arranged for a trustworthy friend to be given power of attorney. My house was completely empty except for the curtains and fitted carpets, and as I walked through the bare rooms on the final day, memories of the years I had lived there began to fill my mind. I had no regrets, I knew I should never look back and wish I had not done it. The Lord gives us the desires of our heart, and I was sure that in His plan lay the highest possibility for joy and fulfilment in my life. I knelt and prayed, 'Dear Father, bless this house and everyone who will ever live here. Lord Jesus, I give You my life, my will, my all. Please teach me and lead me in the paths You have chosen for my life. In Your precious name I pray, Amen.'

I walked out into the weak January sunshine and locked the door of my home for the last time. A new door was opening.

# Chapter Eight

God's ways are strange, yet most wonderful, inscrutable, yet perfect. Nevertheless, we can have complete peace in surrendering to His government for we know that all His works are ruled by one law of love. Ironically, it is often our own actions which cause us more heartache and perplexity so that we identify with Paul's cry, 'I do not understand what I do. For what I want to do, I do not do, but what I hate, I do' (Rom. 7: 15).

I still had a problem which was not simply a thorn but a dagger in my flesh. I had not been able to give up smoking. God had given me a healthy body and now dwelt within that temple by His Holy Spirit, yet I continued to contaminate it with smoke and nicotine. I loathed the smell of it and I hated myself for my weakness, but I did not seem able to give it up completely. I felt as if people were laughing at me, the smoking missionary, and perhaps they were; Satan certainly was. Sometimes I felt bowed down with guilt and condemnation, and as the day of departure had rushed nearer, I had felt a growing sense of failure and inadequacy. What a useless Christian you are, I accused myself bitterly on some occasions. How can you ever hope to glorify God if you can't even stop smoking?

On the evening before I was due to fly, at my last church service, certain members of the congregation came and asked me if I had won the victory over smoking. I had to admit sadly that the habit was still a problem to me. The disapproving looks crushed my spirit, and again I felt a failure before I had even left British soil. I sought the face of the Lord that evening and clung to His unfailing love and forgiveness.

It was a wonderful service. A visiting preacher spoke with

authority and power on the second coming of the Lord Jesus. His message was urgent and unequivocal, seeming to bear a special anointing from God as he called for wisdom in reading the signs of the times and recognising the rise of the Antichrist and mark of the Beast. He had brought a book which had just been published in America and he strongly advised the church to read it, for it contained a truly inspired understanding of Biblical prophecy and the trends in world politics, economy and society which would indicate the imminent return of the Lord.

I had a strong impression that God wanted me to buy the book though these were all quite new concepts to me. Before the end of the service, however, something happened to make the book slip out of my mind. The pastor called me out in front of the congregation and explained that I should be leaving for the Philippine Islands the following day.

'I'm afraid I have to say that in my opinion Isabel is making a great mistake – but that doesn't mean we withdraw our love.' Then, turning to me, he said in a voice all could hear, 'Isabel, you mustn't be too proud to come back home and admit you were wrong.'

I felt as if I could have crawled under the carpet but there was nothing I could say to justify myself or convince them. I was the errant sheep and I could only submit meekly as the elders laid hands on me and prayed for the Lord's blessing and enlightenment.

It was with a sad and heavy heart that I said my goodbyes to everyone – not that I doubted the Lord's leading despite all the negative words, for the Holy Spirit within us bears the only true witness to our standing before Him – but it would have cheered me on my way to have received their support. However, the Lord Himself is a God of encouragement, and one woman stepped forward and handed me a small piece of paper, hugged and assured me of her prayers. Deeply touched, I thanked her and turned aside to open the note. It read, 'The Lord had laid on my heart for you Jeremiah 1 verses 5 to 8.'

I reached for my Bible swiftly and tears pricked my eyes as I saw the words,

'Before I formed you in the womb I knew you, before you were born I set you apart; I appointed you as a prophet to the nations.

"Ah, Sovereign Lord," I said, "I do not know how to speak; I am only a child." But the Lord said to me, "Do not say, 'I am only a child.' You must go to everyone I send you to and say whatever I command you. Do not be afraid of them, for I AM WITH YOU and will rescue you."'

Not one of the Lord's promises has ever failed. With peace in my heart, I made my way towards the door, but the Lord suddenly halted me in my tracks. I felt I *had* to buy the book mentioned earlier in the service, but as I reached for my purse I discovered I had left it behind. Despite the urgency I felt, I persuaded myself that I could leave it, thinking it would probably be like other books I had read. The next second I found myself asking someone if they could lend me the money to buy the book! It seemed God was determined I should read it and, as I was to discover much later, the key to the whole ministry He was leading me into was to be found in its pages.

# Chapter Nine

'Smoking or non-smoking compartment?' barked the steward, mechanically. I had smoked the last cigarette in the packet before entering the plane and I was determined that there would never be another. 'Non-smoking,' I replied in faith and took the seat allocated to me, thankful to be away from the bewildering bustle of Heathrow airport. The place had throbbed with activity, like a huge ant-hill, people rushing to rejoin families and friends, meet deadlines, execute business plans – everyone hurrying towards a definite goal. But as the plane now lumbered heavily along the runway, I realised with a wave of loneliness that there would be no one waiting for me at the end of the journey, no definite work or plan needed my preparation – in fact, I had no imaginable future at all, and I had cut myself off from all my past.

The engines roared as the plane heaved itself off the ground, and as the houses and fields fell away from sight and grey fingers of cloud snaked around the wings, my mind began to fill with fear and doubt. What if my pastor and colleagues were right and I was wrong? I could hear the pastor's words ringing in my ears, 'You mustn't be too proud to come back and admit you were wrong.' You fool, jeered a voice inside me, just look what you've done. You've given up a first-rate job, sold your home, practically given away your furniture for half of what it was worth and you'll never be able to replace it. Just look at you, sitting on this plane, believing that God has called you, but you don't know anything about the country you're going to, you haven't a clue what you'll do when you get there, you don't know a single person, and you can't speak a word of the language . . . On and on the thoughts raged, until my head ached and I was sure I must be crazy. Desperately I reached for my Bible and, when I blindly opened it at random, the first words I read were, 'Trust in the Lord with all your heart and lean not on your own understanding; in all your ways acknowledge Him, and He will make your paths straight' (Prov. 3: 5,6).

The storm within me ceased and I cried quietly, hoping that no one could see or hear me. The Lord knew my thoughts and had sent His Word to bring peace, just as He had done for the disciples on the lake. I began to pray softly under my breath, 'Dear Lord, I am entirely in your hands. I do trust you, but please help me to trust you with *all* of my heart. Teach me, Lord, to turn to you and not to try and work things out for myself. Teach me, Lord, not to make plans for myself. Teach me how to be led by you, Holy Spirit. I love you, Lord Jesus. Amen.'

I leant back in my seat, calm and quiet. I did not know why I was on that plane, but the Lord knew, and He was in control. It is no longer I who live, I thought, but Christ who lives in me. My life is no longer mine to do with as I want. And in the peace that now flooded through my being, His voice came to my heart,

'I will be with you. I will not fail you nor forsake you. Fear not neither be dismayed. My thoughts are not your thoughts, neither are your ways my ways. For as the heavens are higher than the earth, so are My ways higher than your ways and My thoughts than your thoughts.'

Many hours later, the hostess was announcing that we should be arriving in Bangkok in approximately fifteen minutes. Soon the plane landed with a great bump and slid to a halt. Passengers were allowed to disembark for one and a half hours while the plane was refuelling, and we all filed stiffly towards the door. I stepped on to the gangway and was hit by a wall of heat and sunlight. My eyes were dazzled with the brightness of the sun and within thirty seconds the perspiration was running down my body. I could hardly breathe. The bitter cold of the English January I had left seemed to belong to another world and time, and the blue woollen suit I had needed there was soon clinging to my skin. I had never even imagined such heat. I bought a cool, thin dress at the airport terminal, then feeling a little more comfortable, I began to take stock of my surroundings. All about me were dark-skinned people, speaking a strange language, but the atmosphere was friendly, even festive with all the gay colours and lively noise. Suddenly my eye was caught by a young boy standing in a corner selling cigarettes, not in packets, but one or two at a time. The urge to smoke was overwhelming. I battled with the desire, but found myself walking over to the boy and buying one cigarette. The feeling of guilt as I lit it washed me with misery but I had smoked halfway down it before the clear, strong voice of the Lord spoke to my heart, 'This is the day you smoke your last cigarette.'

Stunned, I stared at the cigarette in my hand and was about to take a last puff when I realised the desire was no longer there! It is the *Word* of God alone which sets the captives free. Triumphantly I threw the cigarette away, convinced that I had given up smoking for good and that Satan was under my feet. The Spirit of God made me more than a conqueror! I boarded the plane with a new joy and confidence.

The next stop was Manila, the capital of the Philippines, and my destination. We arrived in the middle of the afternoon and as the door of the plane opened, I was once more engulfed by the appalling heat. For a moment I wondered how I could possibly cope with this temperature but immediately I banished the thought from my mind, remembering that I could do all things through Christ who strengthened me. I picked up my baggage and made my way through immigration.

I must have looked rather lost and forlorn, for a kindly official came over and asked me where I was going. It was on the tip of my tongue to say I didn't know, but realised in time that would not go down very well, so I asked instead for a hotel where I could stay the night if he would kindly find me a taxi. Crisp instructions in Micano, the local language, soon had me speeding through the streets and drawing up outside an extremely grand hotel. They must have thought I was a millionaire not a missionary, I thought wryly to myself, but trusting in the God of abundance to provide rest and comfort, I went inside and soon was climbing wearily between cool, crisp sheets.

I woke next morning with a sense of joy and expectation. Slipping to my knees, I prayed, 'My father in heaven, I hand this day of my life back over to you. I ask you, Lord, to guide me by your Holy Spirit.' I began to pray in tongues and spent the next hour building up my inner self through this heavenly language God had given me, establishing from the start a dependence on the power and supply channelled by this gift.

The hotel staff were excellent and spoke English quite fluently so I was able to find out a little about the island and cash some traveller's cheques. They were also able to tell me how I could make my way to the Miracle Mission at Sanfernando, the address that was my only link with the country. The hotel porter put me in a taxi which bore me, unsuspecting, to my shattering initiation into the wonders of Filipino public transport.

# Chapter Ten

I had managed to communicate with the bus conductor enough to tell him to let me off the bus when we arrived at my destination, and as we drew into another town he pointed at me and said, 'Sanfernando.' I clambered stiffly out across the boxes and crates, and found my suitcases had been dumped by the roadside. Alone, I stood on the side of the street. All I had to do now was find the Mission. I looked for a taxi but could see none, and as I was wondering what to do, a little motor bike with a side car pulled up beside me and a diminutive dark-skinned man jumped off and chattered at me excitedly, flashing a broad white smile. I tried to communicate with him but he only nodded and smiled, gesturing towards the tiny side car. In the end I said, 'Miracle Mission' and that seemed to register, for he nodded even more enthusiastically and seized my suitcase. I decided I might as well follow it, so I climbed into the side car, my suitcase lodged between my left ear and my right foot. We were off at once with a great flourish, rattling and lurching as much as the bus had done, my chauffeur peering down every so often to give an encouraging grin.

Just as I was beginning to wonder if there would be any part of my body not black and blue or permanently disabled, we turned into a steep drive which set the little bike gasping and spluttering, but we managed to crawl breathlessly to the top and coughed to a halt outside a large white building. The noise of the motor bike had broken the peace, and from all directions people and children came hurrying to see what all the commotion was about. In a moment, I was surrounded by excited dark-skinned people, chattering away in their native language so that I felt like an interesting exhibit at a circus. I remembered the photograph of Mercy and, taking it from my purse, I showed it to the nearest group. That caused great excitement, and two or three ran off to return in a few minutes with a woman I immediately recognised as Mercy. It was like meeting an old friend, particularly when I discovered to my joy that she could speak English. But explanations had to be given, and having no clear idea at all why I was there, I just looked at her and said, 'I am here because God has sent me.'

This inspired further animated chatter. I was invited in and given a glass of water, but the big question was not postponed for long. 'Why has God sent you here?' I wished I could have encouraged them with a dynamic revelation of God's plan for me in this country. The puzzled looks at my reply that I simply knew this was where He wanted me to be did not gladden my heart greatly either, and I was not looking forward to my interview with the pastor as they led me down the corridor to his office.

He was a gentle, kindly man, however, standing only as high as my shoulder like most of the small-framed Filipinos, with a broad calm forehead and warm, dark eyes that filled me with confidence. His love for God and for the lost people of his native country irradiated all his words and actions. Now his shrewd gaze penetrated my spirit as he assessed this strange new visitor to the mission. As he asked me particulars of my home and church, it actually struck me for the first time that I had no home at all. The thought crossed my mind that my home was in heaven and I was just passing through, but I could hardly say that. Still, my rather vague replies concerned this good man, and despite the generous welcome he offered me while the Lord revealed His will to us, I could sense He had some reservations about the authenticity of my calling.

The people at the mission were thoughtful and hospitable that day, but a slight barrier remained between us as they pondered in their minds what had inspired this white woman to make the epic journey right across the world without any idea of what she would do when she got there. I was sad, because I could see that I was only an added burden on their already overtaxed resources. But the profound assurance of

God's leading remained with me, and I could only cling to my testimony that He wanted me to be there and had a work for me to do.

At the chapel service that evening, the Lord confirmed His care and provision in the glorious sense of His presence in the worship and in the power of the preaching. My spirit was peaceful. After the service, the faculty head was introduced to me, but I found it difficult to hear what she was saying for my ears had been affected by all the flying and the noise of the bus journey, so we had to abandon the conversation. I was secretly thankful for this temporary deafness as it meant I did not have to keep explaining to people that I did not know why I was there.

The following morning, soon after dawn, I walked around the grounds of the mission. The world seemed to have been reborn, and the clear, fresh light bestowed a jewel-like quality to the panorama spread below. The Mission was situated on the top of a small mountain overlooking the town of Sanfernando and the exotic South China Sea. A few moments in the coolness of the morning convinced me that there was something special about that mountain. The peace of God Almighty was everywhere, resting like a shroud over its tranquil paths and groves. Here and there, picturesque stone steps suggested the olde worlde charm of an English country garden. The ground was parched and dry, yet all around trees and shrubs blazed with colour, their cascading blooms a celebration of irrepressible hope and joy in the barren land. A piece of dead wood, stripped of all leaves and bowing arthritically to the dust, was bedecked with a youthful mantle of bright pink flowers. The Lord God walked in that garden.

The mission comprised an orphanage, which at that time cared for eighty-four children, and a Bible school with approximately seventy students. The children in the orphanage came from heathen villages in the mountains where many of them had seen their parents killed in tribal wars and raids by headhunters. The children were brought to the mission near to death, the victims of a society dominated by witchcraft, demonism, disease and starvation.

If it had not been for the Revd. Clyde Shields's response to the Lord's call to set up the Mission, most of the children would have died, but now, through the grace and healing power of Jesus and the love and practical care ministered by His people, they are healthy, happy, and filled with the Holy Spirit.

The native Bible students had no way of paying for their food and keep, nor their tuition, for they arrived at the Miracle Mission from the mountain provinces with only a small bag of rice to sustain them for the first few days. But each person believed that God was able to provide for their bodies as well as their spirits and at 5.30 every morning the Bible students and the orphans prayed to their Father in heaven to supply all their daily needs.

I went into the town of Sanfernando later in the morning, trying to adjust to the tremendous heat of about a hundred degrees. Mosquitoes seemed to be gnawing every inch of exposed skin and the perspiration soaked my clothes within minutes. I found a market in the centre of the town and walked over to the meat stalls, interested to see what sort of diet the natives lived on. The stench that arose from the piles of sweating meat made me reel. It was just siesta time and suddenly I saw a man on the nearest stall push the meat over to one side, jump on the bench, stretch himself and close his eyes. The flies and insects had a real feast while he slept, and in a second I had made up my mind that I would not eat meat while I was in the country.

All around me, people were settling themselves down and going to sleep in the most extraordinary places. It seemed they simply abandoned what they were doing and lay down on the spot, either on the bench from which they were selling goods, or on the ground in the shade. Along the side of the streets, open drains crawled with the flies and insects which then settled on the meat and fish, and the appalling smell of rotting refuse and sewage made me feel faint and sick.

Children were sitting in the road, throwing stones into the drains, and one child was lying on the ground, scratching his little naked body, listlessly brushing away the flies swarming on his skin. Every so often, a half-starved dog would prowl across the scene, clawing at its flea-infested coat or pulling its bottom along the ground. I wondered how the children could possibly survive in such unhealthy conditions and it did not surprise me to learn later of the soaring infant mortality rate. The homes of the poor people were made of four pieces of corrugated iron, yet in another street only ten minutes' walk away, the detached houses of the wealthy rose cleanly and comfortably above the squalor.

Returning saddened to the mission, I discovered another group of visitors had arrived, an American minister called Revd. Smith and the seven musicians who helped spread the Gospel through song and worship. In the chapel that evening, Revd. Smith began to preach about the power that the believer receives when the Holy Spirit comes upon him or her, and soon he left the pulpit and moved among the students. As he laid hands on them and prayed that they might receive the fullness of the Spirit, an extraordinary thing happened. All of them fell flat on their backs and lay on the ground, some of them shaking from head to foot, others praising God in new languages and raising their hands in adoration, oblivious of everything around. I sat there absolutely stunned, hardly able to believe my eyes and ears. Looking up, I found myself staring straight into the face of the preacher. I could see he was walking towards me and I began to pray furiously, 'Lord, I don't know what's going on here, but please don't let him touch me!'

It was too late. I could feel the preacher's hands on my head and the next moment I was filled with the most wonderful sense of the peace of God, and I heard myself praising Him, singing in the Spirit in a way I had never done before. It was as though I was seated with Christ in heavenly places and I drank in the glory of His splendour. In those moments, He did a precious work in my life for now I had seen the Holy Spirit at work in outward demonstration of His power for the first time.

Revd. Smith and his singing group, men and women from the island itself, were due to leave the mission the following day. I had a strong feeling that the Lord wanted me to join the group, so I went to talk to Revd. Smith about it. I felt daunted by his austere presence as I entered his room rather hesitantly. A tall, stern-faced man in his early sixties, he had a reputation as a hell-fire and brimstone preacher who quoted Scripture with every breath, and although he was not lacking in love, he was inspired more obviously by his zeal for the lost to be saved and come into the reality of God, which he experienced. A man of such determination and directness I knew would view my situation with some suspicion, and I was not surprised when he received me with a certain reserve and formality. It must have been hard for him to accept my story that God had called me to the Philippines without actually telling me why, but after he had fired some sharp, curt questions at me like pistol shots, he curbed his natural disapproval and suggested we seek the Lord concerning my joining the group. He called the others into the room, and when we laid the matter before the Lord in prayer, we were all of one accord. I was to join the group for as long as the Lord led.

## Chapter Eleven

God does not waste time. We spent the next eight days attending a crusade in Manila, and I continually thank the Lord for all He taught me and gave me during that stay. There were three meetings a day, a wealth of Bible teaching, and I spent eight glorious days deep in the Word of God. The people flocked to the Arineta Coliseum and every night hundreds of souls were saved, and we saw the mighty power of the Holy Spirit as people were healed of every kind of illness, disease and affliction through the ministry of Kenneth Copeland.

These meetings gave me a hunger to know more and more about the Bible as I began to understand the power of His Word and the authority that lay in the name of Jesus. I saw that it was by stepping out in faith that we laid hold of that power and authority, bringing release to the captives and sight to those blinded by the lies of Satan. God waited only for that faith-channel for Him to be able to tear down the strongholds of evil and bring in His kingdom. My faith seemed so shallow, but the Lord has promised to equip us with the tools for the work He calls us to, and I knew I just had to banish my doubt and unbelief which prevented my faith from having its full outworking. The Lord had been magnified in my understanding and I had come into a new revelation of His greatness, so I was determined to arm myself for the spiritual battle with all the provision He has made, and open myself to the resources I needed to do His will.

I read Mark 11 verses 23 to 25 and then prayed aloud, 'Lord, I believe that all Scripture is given by your inspiration, written by your prophets as they were moved by your Spirit. I believe that these things your Word speaks about are your will for me. Please, dear Lord, grant me the gift of faith so that I may pray and receive without doubting. Thank you, Father, for the gift of faith!'

The following morning, I awoke and stretched out my hand to pick up my Bible and my spectacles. I slipped on my glasses and opened the Word, but as I began to read the Holy Spirit came upon me and, before I knew what I was doing, I took off my glasses, broke them in two and threw them in the wastepaper basket! The two girls with whom I shared a room stood staring at me in amazement.

'The Lord is going to restore my sight,' I said calmly. My sight had been extremely poor and I had not been able to read anything at all without my glasses. I closed my eyes and prayed, 'Father, I come to you in the name of Jesus. Please heal my eyes and renew my vision. Lord, I believe that when I open my eyes I shall be able to see what is written on the pages before me. Thank you for restoring my sight.'

I looked at the page – and the words seemed to grow in front of me. Black and distinct before my eyes were the wonderful words of Mark 11,

'I tell you the truth,' said Jesus, 'if anyone says to this mountain, "Go, throw yourself into the sea," and does not doubt in his heart but believes that what he says will happen, it will be done for him. Therefore, I tell you, whatever you ask for in prayer, BELIEVE THAT YOU HAVE RECEIVED IT, AND IT WILL BE YOURS.'

In the days that followed, as I confessed my faith in the healing power of His Word, my eyesight steadily improved so that now I can read with my naked eye small print which I had difficulty in reading with my glasses before. In this way, I learnt the precious lesson of receiving the answer to my prayers in my spirit by faith and bringing it into my experience by thanksgiving and confession with the lips. Our bodies are sometimes slow to get the message, but our spirits can minister healing to our flesh by our speaking out in faith the wholeness that is ours in the spiritual realm. In so doing, we are viewing the situation from God's perspective as finished, accomplished, for that is what the Lord Jesus said on the Cross.

Pastor Abbey from Miracle Mission joined us at the end of the convention, having planned a programme of visits to some of the mountain provinces. These were regions into which missionaries seldom ventured, for they were primitive and dangerous for white people. Most of the missionary communities were based in the towns and cities, concentrating on evangelistic campaigns to draw people down from the mountains, or educating born-again Filipinos so that they could go back to their villages and teach the Word of God. The risk to life and health was too great for most missionaries to make the journeys themselves. The villages had not been prepared for our visits, and some were so remote that they had almost no contact with the outside world. Pastor Abbey was to be our guide and interpreter. At first light, we all piled into what the natives called a jeepney, a small truck lined with seats on either side. The seats had no padding and were far from comfortable, and the sides of the truck were open, lending no protection from the heat and dust.

Our destination was a mountain village called Bulalacoa. For the first two hours the journey went tolerably well for the roads were in good condition and there were only the choking heat and the boneshaking seats to contend with. But suddenly the road ended abruptly and continued as a narrow dirt track. Our progress became slow and laboured as the heat of mid-morning beat upon the roof and the track became narrower and more bumpy with every mile. I was sitting at the back of the truck, and as I looked behind us I was amazed that we had been able to pass. Up and up we climbed, the ground becoming drier all the time so that we were soon enveloped in clouds of dust thrown up from the grinding wheels. We had to cover our mouths and noses with handkerchiefs, squinting through streaming half-closed eyelids. My travelling companions had started the journey with jet-black hair and brown faces, but now their hair was grey and their faces covered with a whitish film of dust.

For hour after hour, we crawled up the mountainside, enshrouded by dust, unable to speak and breathing with great difficulty. The dirt track was becoming dangerously narrow, and the wheels of the jeepney were only inches from the edge of the cliff, which dropped sheer down to the valley thousands of feet below us. One false move by the driver, or an unseen stone, and all of us would have gone hurtling down the mountainside into the shallow river which snaked its way so far beneath. I began to pray in gasps through the suffocating dust, Dear Father, protect this jeep. Please be in the wheels, the steering, the brakes. Please keep it on the track. Don't allow it to slip over the edge.

I looked up and saw that all my companions were in prayer also. All at once the jeep came to a standstill. Ahead, the driver had spotted that part of the track was eroded away as if a giant had taken a bite out of the mountainside. It was impossible to turn the jeep around and go back, and I, for one, did not relish the idea of attempting to reverse down the treacherous slope. If the brakes failed ... But I stopped myself abruptly. What was I doing, thinking so negatively? Only a few minutes before I had asked the Lord to take care of the truck, yet I was immediately allowing my heart to be full of fear and doubt. The Lord brought a Scripture to my mind, 'God hath not given us the spirit of fear; but of power, and of love, and of a sound mind' (2 Tim. 1:7 KJV). With His love within me I had no reason to be governed by anxiety. I began to speak to the source of the fear, which was the Devil, 'Spirit of fear and doubt, I command you to leave me in the name of Jesus Christ!'

With a new peace and confidence, I joined the others who had got out of the jeep to examine the road and discuss what could be done. Since the only real course of action was to press on, we laid hands on the jeep and prayed that if the road was not wide enough then the Lord in His mighty power would carry us past the crumbled part of the road. To encourage the driver, and our own spirits, we began to sing, and as the jeep edged closer and we continued to rejoice, all fear seemed to vanish. The next thing I heard was shouts of 'Hallelujah!' and I saw we were safely on the other side. The driver said that only part of the wheels on the inside had had ground underneath but the biggest part of the wheels had been balancing in mid-air! I blessed the Lord with all my heart, not only for the miracle, but also for the fact that He had so completely freed me from fear. I knew that only a few months ago I could never have undertaken such a journey.

The scenery, when we could see it through the clouds of dust, was quite breathtaking. Range after range of mountains marched into the purple distance and every so often a river would glint from deep in a valley, or a jungle area would burst upon our sight with exotic colours and rich shades of green. Hours ago we had passed a sign saying '7,400 feet' and I could not imagine how much higher we had climbed since then. Finally, the pastor announced that we were approaching a village where we should be able to get something to eat. We had been on the road for six hours and there were at least another three before we would reach our destination. I went with my female companions to what the natives called the 'comfort room' or public lavatories, which turned out to be a corrugated iron erection with a single drain. The stench was appalling and there was no privacy, but neither was there any choice, so pride had to be subdued and I performed the same ritual as the other girls, then staggered, gasping, into the bright sunlight.

I longed for somewhere to wash off the dust with which I was covered from head to foot. My ears were blocked and I could not tell if it was with dirt or because of the high altitude. I was filthy, hot, thirsty and hungry, but one look at the porridge-like concoction the Filipinos were eating took away my appetite, and I took a drink from an old enamel mug, rusted with age, which had been passed round to everyone. I was glad when we all climbed back into the jeep and I naively looked forward to the bath and decent meal awaiting us at the end of our journey.

At last we arrived. The jeep pulled up outside a little home made of bamboo, sitting on top of four small stilts. The occupants came hurrying out at the sound and greeted us with great warmth and love, evidently overjoyed at seeing us. The lady of the house ushered the girls indoors into a tiny room which had just one single bed in it – and that had no mattress. Surprise and acute disappointment swept over me and my jaw must have dropped, for my companions suddenly began to laugh at my expression. For a moment I felt hurt and angry. I was dirty, exhausted, ravenous, and my bones ached with sitting on that hard seat for nine hours – and the bed did not even have a mattress! I could not see what they were finding so funny.

But the situation was so awful that one could only laugh or cry. So I began to laugh and found myself laughing and laughing until my sides ached even more and the tiny room rocked with gales of amusement from us all. Tears streamed down our faces, mingling with the dust so that we looked like circus clowns. Eventually we pulled ourselves together and decided to make the most of our predicament. We were there to do the work of the Lord and would be able to cope with any situation in His strength.

My next discovery was that the only means of washing was a tap situated in the middle of the yard in full view of everyone. I wet my handkerchief under it and began to wipe off the dust and grime which coated the outside of my small travelling case containing a few changes of clothes. The case had given little protection: every garment was filled with dust. I shook each one and reconciled myself to the fact that dirt was something that must be accepted and I decided to bid farewell to my Western refinement. Four pieces of corrugated iron were fixed up around the tap and one by one the girls began to wash themselves. It was nearly dark by the time my turn came. I knelt on the ground and laboriously washed my hair under a slow trickle of water, and then washed my body, all the time ducking down below the level of the metal walls. It was an ordeal, for being white-skinned made me quite a novelty among the natives, and I was aware of being watched constantly.

Night had fallen thickly on the small community perched on the mountainside. One kerosine lamp provided poor light for the meal which had been prepared, and I could not see what I was eating, but I was hungry and devoured the rice and whatever else was put in front of me. There were no knives, forks or spoons so I soon adopted the native style of holding the plate close to my mouth and shovelling the food in with my fingers.

After eating, we retired for the night, and by the light of the small torch I had brought, the Filipino girls and I undressed in the tiny room no more than ten feet by twelve. The only piece of furniture was the wooden bed and two of us slept on that while the others lay on the floor. We were all worn out by the travelling, but before sleeping we prayed together and thanked the Lord for getting us there safely, for the food we had been given and for the water which had refreshed us. God had provided for all our needs and we slept peacefully in moments.

In the morning, I went to the makeshift 'bathroom' and cleaned my teeth, surrounded by a circle of solemn brown faces. The local children had never seen a white woman before, let alone one who filled her mouth with strange white foam from a long plastic instrument. At once I became a star attraction, followed everywhere by a trailing line of giggling, pointing urchins. Although I could not communicate with them, I soon made friends with one or two of the bolder ones. The others hung back, staring with their beautiful black eyes, occasionally daring to touch my dress or put a curious hand on my straight brown hair.

Another spectator was the pig which roamed grunting around the door of the washroom, the end of its rope tied to one of the stilts upon which the house was built. Hens and ducks darted about our legs but were happiest sitting under the shade of the table where the meals were eaten. This was also the favourite haunt of flies, and clouds of them had to be shooed away when the food was laid out.

We held meetings on both the evenings we were there, although few of the villagers turned up. Witchcraft, superstition and fear held many in bondage and made it hard for them to make a stand in front of family and friends. Two people repented of their sin, however, and asked Jesus into their hearts, so we knew the kingdom of darkness had been shaken.

# Chapter Twelve

The next day we were up at the crack of dawn, preparing to leave for our second destination which was another village called Polasaan. There was no road to this village so our journey was continued on foot, hiking along a narrow mountain track. The walk took four hours as we trudged along heavily, carrying our baggage on our shoulders or native-style on our heads. My own attempts were awkward and clumsy, while the Filipinos travelled with ease and grace.

The scorching sun beat down on us, and even though we reached Polasaan before the sweltering heat of midday I still got very sunburnt. Despite my beetroot colour, however, I did not blister or suffer any discomfort and the burn soon mellowed to a deep brown and provided a screen against the sun on subsequent hikes.

Our lodging place was built of corrugated iron, but this time it was big enough to sleep everyone more comfortably. The domestic facilities were no better but I was discovering that the Filipino people were extremely hospitable and went to great lengths to ensure that we were given as much comfort as their primitive conditions would allow. The pastor of the village and his wife were excellent hosts. We had planned to stay for three days, holding a meeting each evening, but the villagers begged us to stay an extra night for it soon became clear that God was moving in a remarkable way.

The first evening, the music group started by singing praises to God in choruses which the natives were quick to pick up. Then to my surprise, I was asked to address the congregation with Pastor Abbey as interpreter. I stood up and found myself facing a vast sea of brown faces, curious and expectant. My mind went completely blank and panic seized me as I thought of how unqualified and unprepared I was to teach these people. But suddenly the words came to me, '"Be not afraid of their faces: for I am with thee to deliver thee," saith the Lord' (Jer. 1:8KJV).

I stopped thinking about my inadequacy and fixed my eyes on the God of all power who is able to do immeasurably more than all we ask or imagine (Eph. 3:20). Opening my mouth, trusting that He would supply the words, I suddenly found a message pouring from my lips about the imminent return of Jesus Christ and warning against the rise of the Antichrist and the mark of the Beast. It seemed a strange word to give these primitive mountain folk, but it was a message that came not from my own mind but from the Spirit of God, whose presence seemed to descend like a cloud upon the meeting.

As I finished, Revd. Smith stood and explained the need to be set free from the bondage of sin and to receive the glorious gift of eternal life that had been won for each person by the death and resurrection of Jesus. The atmosphere was electric. The whole congregation swarmed forward and with one accord these primitive people knelt and repented of their sins, turning from the witchcraft and worship of idols that had ruled their lives and acknowledging Jesus Christ as the one true Lord and Saviour.

The sight of one woman crying quietly moved me deeply, and I went over to comfort her. As I laid my hand on her shoulder, I was amazed to see her instantly fall to the ground and lie there motionless. I did not really know what was happening, but God was evidently powerfully at work so I knelt beside her and asked the Lord to fill her with His Holy Spirit. I left her lying on the floor with her hands raised, praising God ecstatically in a new heavenly language. I was then led to a man and, as I placed my hand on him, the power of God again came down and he too fell flat on his back and received the gift of tongues as I prayed for the Holy Spirit to fill him.

To one after another the same thing happened and eventually I stood back and took stock of the situation. The place looked like a battlefield. Revd. Smith and the other members of the group were also praying for the villagers and the floor was covered with people lying on their backs, worshipping God in dozens of languages, some shaking from head to foot as the Holy Spirit reached deep into their lives and touched the areas that needed healing or deliverance. Elsewhere people were dancing up and down with joy, radiant gladness transforming their faces. As I knelt to thank the Lord for revealing Himself to us in such a powerful way, a profound peace came upon me, the peace of God which passes all understanding. We had seen the hand of God, performing wonders according to His promises, and He was drawing me into the ministry He had prepared. Each night, more and more people came to the meetings and hundreds of souls found new life and hope.

During the afternoon of the second day, we decided to visit some of the families who had not come to the meeting the previous night. One home in particular belonged to a retired couple who were strikingly different from most of the impoverished people in that community. They lived in a substantial concrete house set apart from the rest of the village, and we soon discovered that they owned two gold mines near by.

The couple invited us into their grand home where the group sang choruses and we testified to the love of Jesus for them, and the salvation that was available through His forgiveness. The message touched their hearts, and as they knelt to repent of their sins and ask Jesus to become Lord of their lives, we laid hands on them and asked God to fill them with His Holy Spirit. What happened next was a surprise to everyone. Suddenly I found myself shouting at the man of the house, 'Out, out, out!' Everyone stared at me, amazed, but the man got up at once and returned in a few seconds carrying a china statue of Buddha. He gestured to his wife to open the window shutter, then threw the figure headlong into the garden where it smashed into a thousand pieces. None of us had had any idea that the couple were worshippers of Buddha, but the Holy Spirit knew – and He had not yet finished His refining work in this house. The next moment I was walking from room to room, casting out evil spirits in the name of Jesus Christ as the Holy Spirit led. I would never have dreamt of shouting at a man in his own home, nor of walking boldly through each room exorcising spirits, but God knew that these people were under the influence of the Devil, and I was merely the instrument He used to set them free. I opened my Bible and read,

> You shall have no other gods before me. You shall not make for yourself an idol in the form of anything in heaven above or on the earth beneath or in the waters below. You shall not bow down to them or worship them; for I, the *Lord* your God, am a jealous God (Exod. 20:3-5).

Nothing is hidden from God. The Holy Spirit convicts, not condemns, and this man knew the joy of liberation and the complete forgiveness that is given through the Lord's abundant mercy and love.

Something had stirred in our hearts when we heard of the people who worked in the gold mines deep in the mountain, and we asked the Lord to guide us if He wanted us to take His gospel to them. It was arranged that we should get up at dawn the next morning, and make our descent into the valley before the crippling heat of midday.

No one had mentioned just how steep or dangerous the journey would be. Standing on the edge of an almost sheer cliff, we gazed silently into the cavernous mouth of a great gully, watching the ant-like figures dragging their burdens out of the rock face a thousand feet below. We thought of God's promise, 'He will command His angels concerning you to guard you in all your ways; they will lift you up in their hands, so that you will not strike your foot against a stone' (Ps. 91: 11-12).

That cheered me, for I had never climbed so much as a hundred feet down a crumbling mountainside, and a head for heights had never been my strongest point.

Before starting the descent, we knelt and prayed. 'Our Father in heaven, we come to you in the name of Jesus, asking that your guardian angels will be especially alert and that you will guide our every step. We claim that you will safeguard each one of us from any accident or injury, and that you will empower us to do your work and to climb back safely to the top of this mountain.'

Slowly we began the long, hot climb into the very bowels of the earth. After about half an hour of creeping like flies across a wall, my nerve began to falter under the attack of insidious little thoughts. 'No one in his right mind would attempt such a climb without safety ropes,' protested a voice in my head. 'You really are crazy, Isabel. Your boss was right, you *do* need a psychiatrist! Any minute now your foot will slip and you'll go hurtling down this treacherous cliff like a big boulder. They'll bury you at the bottom of this mountain and you'll never be heard of again.'

My legs began to shake and I tried to sit down, but there was only enough room for my feet. I leant against the mountain, pressing my face to the warm rock, trying to blot out the sight of the formidable descent below. Sand began to crumble under my feet and trickle down the mountainside. You'd better move quickly, I told my paralysed legs, or the piece of rock you're standing on will collapse under your weight. Panic seized me, but then I remembered our prayer and recognised that this was the old enemy trying to fill my mind with fear so that I lost control and plunged to my death.

'Devil,' I said loudly, 'in the name of Jesus, get out of my mind and take your negative thoughts with you!'

That did it. I began to sing and moved forward, rejoicing in the victory and the love of Jesus which casts out all fear. In places there were only a few inches of cracked rock on which to place our feet, the heat and savage mosquitoes bombarded our flesh, and near the end my legs began to tremble as though the muscles would give way, and I scrambled the last hundred feet on all fours. We all reached the bottom safely. Hot and thirsty, we exulted at the sight of a clear refreshing spring, and within seconds we were splashing our faces and drinking in huge gulps from the cold bright water.

The miners had been watching our descent with curiosity

and some incredulity. A small crowd had gathered to meet us, overjoyed at having visitors, a rare thing when such a treacherous mountain face separated them from the outside world. There were three different mines, and therefore three distinct communities in this forgotten valley, but the people were united by a common worship of idols and of the sun or moon. When we began to tell them about our God, God the Father, God the Son, and God the Holy Spirit, they grew angry and started to shout at us to keep away from their mines. They feared that their gods would be filled with wrath if they listened to another god, and would not show them where to find gold. Their anger became so violent that we had to leave the first group and move out of sight, but the foreman of the third mine invited us to go over there.

The mine head was a gaping gash in the mountainside, quarried by hand by men with shovels and picks; no machinery had ever been seen in that remote spot. Generations had toiled to their deaths in these mines, men pitting their strength against the hard rock, gouging out great pieces which were shovelled into wheelbarrows and pushed laboriously through the darkness in the back-breaking tunnels, out into the blinding sunlight. There women waited, crouching like vultures over the piles of ore and stone. Week after week, month after month, year after year, these women sat on their haunches, their skin scorched and toughened by the tropical sun until it looked like elephant hide, mechanically turning over the lumps of rock that rained from the wheelbarrows, or chipping at the larger pieces with small picks to see if there was gold at the centre.

We were invited to look inside the mine, which was simply a tunnel piercing deep into the heart of the mountain. Bent almost double, we shuffled painfully along the rock-strewn ground. Only the leader carried a light, and for minutes at a time I would be in complete darkness, straining to breathe in the intense heat, the distant sound of hammering sounding like the earth's heartbeat. There was little oxygen, and the sense of pressure that this produced made me think of the millions of tons of mountain on top of us. Quickly I called on the name of Jesus to overcome the fear that began to rise and I whispered into the darkness, 'Jesus, I love you and I have nothing to fear.'

On and on we dragged ourselves, until finally we came to the end of the tunnel and the guide raised his lamp to show us a piece of rock which had a bright golden streak through it, but many men had sold their souls for this lie. This was not real but 'fool's gold'. Only one or twice a year they found real gold, and sometimes they would dig for years without finding any. How small its value seemed then in comparison with the cost of human lives and happiness.

By the time we emerged into the brilliant sunshine which seemed like a whiplash across our eyes, our lungs were bursting. But by going into the mine we had gained the workers' confidence. Now, in the shade of the mine entrance, we were able to sit down on pieces of rock and explain to these primitive miners that there was only one true God, who was the Creator of the heaven and the earth, the sun and moon and all the stars. The God we worshipped brought the light every morning and the darkness every night. He refreshed the land with dew and rain so that the crops grew and we had food and water. Everything that was ever made was created by our God, who loved them and had sent us to tell them of His love.

They listened with wondering, rapt attention, amazed to hear of a God who ruled by love not fear, and who *gave* instead of demanding sacrifice. Our time had run out, but we explained that we should be having a meeting at the top of the mountain that evening, and if they came they would hear more of the Saviour of the world. We invited them to climb back with us, but they laughed and said they had been climbing that mountain since they were able to walk, 'You are too slow for us,' they said with amusement. 'When you are near the top we shall begin climbing.'

I had not been looking forward to the upward climb, but I prayed for the Lord's strength to reach the top and, although the last one to begin, I was the first to reach the summit, climbing with a supernatural strength and ease far above my own ability.

That evening at the service many of the miners were present and came forward for prayer to receive salvation and be filled with the Holy Spirit. They were set free from the hopelessness and misery induced by the arduous toil and repressed belief in fickle gods, and they agreed to come and find out more about this merciful Saviour at the weekly meetings held by the local pastor.

We were meant to be leaving the following day, but once more the natives pleaded with us to stay, and our love for our new brothers and sisters in Christ made it impossible to refuse. It enabled me to learn another important lesson. Up there in the mountains where the natives practised voodoo and witchcraft, we were aware that we were surrounded by evil spirits, for the presence of wickedness became almost a tangible force at times and we were conscious of persistent attack in many areas. But we knew that as we rested in Christ and armed ourselves with His authority, nothing could harm us – so I was surprised when I awoke the following morning to feel a pain across my shoulders which made it difficult to move my head. I put it down to the discomfort of sleeping on the hard bamboo and expected it to ease off, but, as the day progressed, the pain became more intense and I asked Revd. Smith to pray for me. Sensing by the Holy Spirit that the cause of the pain was demonic, he rebuked the evil spirit and told it to leave in the name of Jesus Christ. Instantly the pain left and I was never troubled with it again.

Day by day, my faith had been growing by demonstrations of God's power such as this, and I had come to the realisation that there was no limit to what could be done in the name of Jesus. It could not be explained with the rational mind, but I knew in my heart that whatever the problem, Jesus was the answer; the Word of God promised it, and faith in that promise proved it.

On the afternoon of that last day, I found a young girl about fourteen years old sitting on the ground, hiding behind a rock, sobbing as if her heart would break. She heard me coming towards her and ran away at once, so I sent two Filipino girls to look for her. Eventually they brought her to the pastor's house and through an interpreter I asked her to tell me why she was so sad. I was shocked by the child's nervous and tearful explanation. Five spirits dressed in black robes controlled her life. In one hand they held a rope and in the other a stick. She was very frightened of them, but she could never escape because they were with her all the time and threatened her if she did not obey them. I asked her where they were now, and she said they could not come into the pastor's house, but they were waiting for her outside. We laid hands on the poor girl and began to pray in the name of Jesus, but she began screaming that they were still there and would never leave her.

Then, all at once, someone noticed that she had a string of black beads around her neck. When we asked her to remove them, she grasped them tightly, crying wildly that if she took them off something terrible would happen to her. Evidently there was an evil spell at work on this child, and the hold was in the beads. But how could she be convinced to take them off? Many, many minutes of gentle persuasion and encouragement were necessary before she reached up and removed the beads with trembling hands. Immediately the control that these spirits had over her life was broken and we bound and cast them out in the name of Jesus. She began to cry uncontrollably and, when she finally grew quiet, she looked up with a new peace and serenity, the terrified, hunted expression banished from her eyes. She repented of her sins and asked Jesus to fill her with His Spirit. It had been years since she laughed like a normal child. Now she was radiant with the joy of belonging to Jesus.

## Chapter Thirteen

It was difficult to say goodbye to our new-found family in Palasaan, but we parted knowing that if we never saw each other again on this earth, we should definitely spend eternity together in the house of the Lord. For Jesus Himself said, 'In My Father's house are many mansions ... I go to prepare a place for you' (John 14:2 KJV).

Our next destination was a place called Tabuk Kalingo-Apayao where we were to be the guests of Revd. and Mrs Teckney. We arrived weary and travel-stained and were overjoyed to find a room with two single beds which even had mattresses. After sleeping on a hard bamboo floor for a couple of weeks, a soft bed seemed sheer luxury, and my delight was made complete by the sight of a proper washroom in complete privacy, even though there was no running water. After a meal and a wash, we retired for the night, and as I wriggled contentedly into the welcoming sheets, I blessed the Lord for His leading which had brought me such a deep appreciation of such basic comforts. I drew the mosquito net over me and drifted to sleep, reflecting thankfully that for the first time I should spend a night unbitten by vicious insects.

My sleep was sweet and I rose relaxed and refreshed for a breakfast of boiled rice and aubergines. By now I had grown accustomed to eating without questioning whatever was put in front of me. I learnt not to eat 'with my eyes', but to fill my stomach. Some of the concoctions the natives served left much to be desired, often a matted pottage of rice and vegetables, cooked all together in a metal pan resting on two stones over a fire made of dried coconut husks. Meat in the mountain provinces was almost unheard of, except for the occasional dog, rat or snake. But on very special occasions a chicken would be killed. Nothing was wasted, not even the intestines which were considered, in fact, a great delicacy. I remember one day I found something in my mouth which had a bitter flavour and a strange, rubbery texture. I swallowed it with difficulty and asked the interpreter what I was eating. He explained that as the honoured guest, I had been given the intestines as this was the most delicate part of all. My stomach heaved and the mouthful I had just eaten came back into my mouth. Somehow I managed to swallow it down again, for I knew that if I had got up and spat it out, the natives would have been deeply offended, and I should have destroyed the confidence and trust I was building up with them. That was the last time I ever asked what I was eating. Thereafter I simply prayed that the Lord would bless the food to my body, and then ate with a thankful heart.

After breakfast, Pastor Teckney invited me to sit with him and I joined him willingly, never imagining the dramatic revelation that would take place. Quietly, this gentle and wise man of God explained that for twelve years he and the believers in that area had been praying that the Lord would send them a missionary with whom they would go into the mountains and preach the gospel to the *headhunters*. I was silent, trying desperately not to see the implication of what he was saying, so he looked at me intently and asked, 'Why are you here, Isabel?' his deep dark eyes scanning my face thoughtfully. 'A white woman in these parts is almost unheard of.'

'I really don't know, Pastor,' I replied patiently, as I had done so many times before, 'except that God has led me here in a remarkable way. But . . . ' and suddenly I found myself telling this godly man that Jesus was coming back soon and I was here to warn the people about following the False Messiah instead of the one true Christ. I had had no intention of saying all this at all but I found to my astonishment that the words just came tumbling out under the direct inspiration of the Holy Spirit. When I had finished telling him of the message God had laid upon my heart, Pastor Teckney sat perfectly still with his eyes closed fast for what seemed an age. I even began to wonder if he had fallen asleep.

At length, he looked up and said gravely, 'Isabel, I believe what you have said is from God. I have just seen a great shaft of golden light ... ' I blinked in surprise for the room had remained just the same to me. 'I believe the Lord showed me that tremendous light as an assurance and proof that what you are saying is true, and that you have been sent here by the Lord to help us go into the mountains and preach His Word.' He stood up, a new brightness in his eye, and added, 'Please don't be influenced by what I have said. Continue to pray and be led by the Holy Spirit. He will guide you in God's perfect will for us all.'

I spent the rest of that day studying the Word of God, but in the evening I was still unsure of the course of action I should take. The idea of trying to pacify angry headhunters with the message of Jesus's love did not fill me with enthusiasm and I longed to stay with my Filipino travelling companions who had so generously taken me to their heart in this lonely country. When I talked with them, it seemed so sensible that we should all return to the Miracle Mission together at the end of the week as planned, for we had been united in a common goal which now seemed near fulfilment. Besides this, our financial resources were running very low and I had not brought my passport, so had no means of cashing money and staying on independently. To leave seemed the wisest plan – and yet, complete peace eluded me.

We held a couple of services but they were very dry compared with the meetings which had gone before, and there was a general feeling that the Holy Spirit was being held back. Revd. Smith and his music group finalised their plans to return to the Mission, but in my heart I had a growing conviction that I should not accompany them. Again I took the situation to my Father in heaven, at last laying down my own desires at His feet and opening myself honestly to His leading.

'Should I stay here, Lord, and take your Word up to the mountain tribes, or do you want me to continue with my brothers and sisters and return to the mission?' As I prayed, I remembered my impoverished state, and found myself adding, 'Father, you know I have no papers or identification with me at all, and I can't stay here without some money to pay my expenses and journey back to the Mission alone. If you want me to stay, please allow my traveller's cheques to be cashed here at the local bank.' It was a tall order, for the tiny bank in this remote spot had probably never seen a traveller's cheque and would certainly be wary of handing over money to a foreigner with no identification. But I knew God was able to do anything.

Susan Teckney, the pastor's daughter, took me down into the little town and we entered a ramshackle hut that bore no sign of being a building of any importance or authority – except for the two fearsome guards standing incongruously outside armed with guns. Susan explained in the native language to the man behind the makeshift grill that I needed some cash but had left my passport and documents at Sanfernando. A conversation between the assistant and the bank 'manager' resulted in a few questions from this lofty gentleman in his broken English and then, without any fuss, they calmly cashed the cheques and waved us a cordial farewell. We went on our way, rejoicing at this miracle which proved so conclusively that the Lord's will was for me to remain and go up to the headhunters with the message of His love.

Revd. Smith and the others rose at five next morning to start their long journey back to the Mission, and there was sadness in my heart as I embraced each one and watched them disappear in the darkness of the early morning. I had grown to love them deeply, having shared a wonderful time of fellowship together and seen a tremendous move of the Holy Spirit. I had learnt important lessons of faith through the spiritual dynamism of Revd. Smith, and in subsequent days I saw the provision of the Lord which had trained and disciplined me to be able to walk on with Him alone.

I spent the next few days resting and studying the Bible, much of which was still unexplored territory to me, and I devoured its pages hungrily, thrilled at the wealth of promises given to us by a faithful God and loving heavenly Father. Salvation seemed the very minimum He offered as I read of the abundant life Jesus came to bring, and the power, wholeness, joy and health available to us *now* through faith. It was only later that I realised how blessed I was in having nothing to 'unlearn', no preconceptions or prejudices to overcome. God's Word was exciting and new, and I saw no reason to question or doubt any of His promises for I had never known Him to fail.

How could there be any problem that was insuperable for the Creator of the universe? I *expected* healing when I prayed for those who were sick; I *expected* deliverance for those who were in spiritual bondage; I *expected* all my physical and financial needs to be met because I took as my yardstick, as the *truth* concerning the situation, God's Word, and not human reason and limitations. I understood what was meant by a 'fool for Christ' and what it was to be a child before Him, for I was used to being mocked for the 'irrationality' of my actions when following His leading. I was aware, too, of my ignorance of theological concepts and the intricacies of Bible history. But what did it matter when He had promised to provide the words and the wisdom for every situation and not only that, but to supply all our practical needs too? What freedom from anxiety and fear He offered! His wisdom did not depend on intellect or learning, but was mediated through His Holy Spirit, and His provision was not restricted to our human resources.

One day, opening my Bible at random, I read,

Finally, be strong in the Lord and in His mighty power. Put on the full armour of God so that you can take your stand against the devil's schemes. For our struggle is not against flesh and blood, but against the rulers, against the authorities, against the powers of this dark world and against the spiritual forces of evil in the heavenly realms (Eph. 6:10-12).

The Lord had been teaching me much about the spiritual battle that we are fighting, and these words confirmed my own experience as I recalled the times I had been attacked by a spirit of fear, and how, when I had prayed in the name of Jesus, it had left. These things are difficult to understand with the human mind for it is so easy to attribute all problems to a psychological or emotional root, all social unrest to political or economic factors, thus missing the deeper cause which lies in the spiritual realm. But God's Word says that our fight is against the devil and his evil host, therefore pain, sickness, disease, violence and all suffering are provoked by these powers of darkness. I believed it. It was enough for me to know that over all these evil forces, authority is given to every believer to free from bondage the oppressed and to establish the peace and wholeness of God's kingdom. I was to need that power and assurance in the days to come.

As we sat round the table after supper one evening, Pastor Teckney began to tell me about the Bute Bute tribe, the headhunters who lived in the near-by mountain ranges. Weird and savage tribal customs still ruled these primitive people. When they elected a new chief, the chosen warrior had to prove that he was worthy of the honour by killing someone from another tribe at dead of night and bringing back the head as a trophy. Their marriage ceremonies were similarly barbaric. At certain times of the year, the chosen bridegroom had to murder a member of another tribe, and present the head to the wife-to-be as proof of his virility and courage; no head, no bride. When young boys reached puberty, they were sent out on headhunting raids, and when they returned with their prizes the tribe accepted that they had passed from boyhood to manhood and were worthy of the status of warriors. Tribal wars raged in the mountains and in certain areas it would be suicide to venture in, but there were other parts which were relatively safe except for the occasional ritual murder.

As Pastor Teckney described these things, my heart began to beat very fast and goose-pimples prickled all over my body. I knew it was God's will that we should enter the headhunters' territory and He was able to remove all fear of what lay before us.

## Chapter Fourteen

Satan sometimes lacks subtlety. The following morning, news came that during the night headhunters had visited this very town, Tabuk, and a dead body had been found with the head savagely cut off. Suddenly the terrifying stories became an ugly reality but, instead of being deterred from our expedition, I was filled with a deep compassion for the blindness of these people, bound to customs that had been practised in their tribes for generations. They needed to know about the grace and peace of Jesus which could set them free from such a violent system. The Holy Spirit was the only power which could reveal to them the error of their customs, for no human reasoning could ever convince them. We decided to fast and pray to seek the Lord's guidance about our mission.

We had good reason to trust in God's love and concern for these barbaric tribes. Next day, Pastor Teckney told us of an occasion when the Lord had moved in a mighty way. Some local Christians had gone a little way into the mountain districts some time before, and had spread the gospel. A handful of natives had accepted the Lord Jesus as their Saviour and, as the Holy Spirit began to work in their lives, they left the Bute Bute tribe and moved with their families to a completely different area, digging out new rice paddies and building bamboo houses for themselves. As the years passed, the children grew, and in turn gave birth to another generation to which the parents and grandparents witnessed about the love of Jesus. They built a native church, which was roofed with straw, and there they worshipped and praised their God daily.

Pastor Teckney described how during one of his visits to this village, when there was particular unrest among the tribes, they arose after the midday siesta to see in the distance a tribal war party approaching, hideously slashed with war paint and armed with cruel spears and knives. The villagers were overwhelmed with grief, for they knew they would be attacked and many of their loved ones killed. They refused to run and they would not fight, but decided instead to trust in God and accept whatever He brought. The war party drew nearer, then halted, waiting for dark to provide the cover for their raid. The villagers went into their makeshift church, got down on their knees and prayed and waited. Darkness was upon them and still they prayed and waited. Gradually, their prayer changed to praise and soon they were praising God in a way they had never known before. Hours had passed, and still no attack. Eventually they all left the church in complete darkness, went to their huts and rested for a few hours, returning before the light of dawn, for as the attack had not come in the night, they thought the strategy of the other tribe was to fall on the village with the light of a new day. Again they began to praise God with joy in their hearts. Still nothing happened. As the God of the universe rolled back the darkness of night and touched the earth with the light of morning, the villagers could see no sign of the war party. A search was instigated, and all that was found were two young warriors hiding in the bushes on the outskirts of the village. Their tribe had decided to attack as night fell, but through the darkness they suddenly saw hundreds of lighted torches burning all round the village. It seemed that a huge force was preparing to fight against them, and in fear and disarray they had decided to retreat. The two young men could not explain why they had not gone back with the company. It could only be that the Spirit of God had been drawing them. The villagers could hardly believe their ears as they knew that everyone had been on their knees in the church. God had obviously placed his angels round the village to ward off attack just as He promised in Psalm 34 verse 7, 'The angel of the Lord encamps around those who fear him, and he delivers them.'

The young warriors who had been found were so astounded by this explanation that they received Jesus as their Saviour and were filled with the Holy Spirit.

What a tale this was to enlarge our vision of God's sovereignty over every situation! We spent the rest of the evening in prayer and praise for the miracles we believed God would perform, sleeping that night with the peace of God ruling in our hearts about the expedition that was to commence next morning.

The first streaks of dawn in the east revealed the silent figures of our team preparing our baggage and provisions for the long journey into the mountain provinces of Northern Luzon. There were just six of us: our guide, two local boys to act as baggage carriers, Pastor Teckney, his daughter, Susan, and me. One of the boys carried a guitar for Susan to play. Being Filipinos, the pastor and his daughter had some knowledge of the tribal dialect, but I was still completely dependent on their interpreting and on the Holy Spirit.

We travelled as far as possible by jeep along the rough roads, and when these petered out, a pony and cart carried us along a dirt track until we came to the first river, where we were forced to continue on foot. The brown water swirled round our legs, reaching up to our waists in places as we pushed against the current, our baggage precariously balanced on our heads. The river bordered on to flooded rice paddies, criss-crossed with a network of narrow mud dykes just a few inches wide. I tried to walk along these ridges, because dragging my feet through the mud soon sapped my legs of strength, but I kept slipping on to the oozing field. Time and again, my shoes got stuck in the mud, so I decided I should do better to carry my shoes and go barefoot as the natives did. But first I claimed the Lord's protection as I knew that the rice paddies were infested with blood-sucking leeches which fixed themselves to the leg or foot so firmly that if one was pulled off a lump of skin would be torn off with it. It was a question of simply waiting until the creature had sucked as much blood as its body could hold and then it fell back into the water. Not one of these leeches ever touched my skin, though I knew the natives accepted them as part of life.

The temperature was over a hundred degrees. As the sun beat down and we stumbled on through the rice paddies and rocky paths, the perspiration streamed down my body in rivulets. On and on we hiked, until after four hours we approached some sort of rough building. My vision was blurred, for my eyes were clouded with sweat and dirt, but as we drew closer, I saw that it was a native home. It was no more than a hut, only providing the most basic shelter from the fierce heat of the sun. I noticed other dwellings high above us, dotted around a clearing which was on a terrace of ground dug out hundreds of years ago by the tribe's ancestors. This was the ancient world of the headhunters. The primitive village was set into the mountainside on series of tiny plateaux, with the rice fields similarly gouged out of the hill into flat terraces. It seemed like a Stone Age community, and I discovered later that their only tools were indeed made of stone, and their speech and culture were equally primitive.

The pastor told us to smile and wave to indicate that we were friendly and did not mean them any harm. Out of the primeval dwellings emerged people who made me rub my eyes in disbelief. The children were naked, and so were the parents and old people too, except for the occasional loincloth. One native man offered us a drink from an earthenware vessel as a gesture of goodwill, and we all drank solemnly.

As we passed more solitary huts, the children ran behind us and began to shout excitedly, 'Perau! Perau! Perau!' I asked the interpreter what 'perau' meant and he replied, 'white'. They had never seen a woman with white skin before. We ascended to the main part of the village, the crowd growing as people caught the cry of 'perau!' and soon we were surrounded by staring faces. I looked round at the wall of pressing bodies, and was shocked and sickened by what I saw. Their skin was covered with rough tattoos which had obviously been carved into the skin with blunt, dirty instruments, for many of them had not healed and were running with pus or caked with scabs. Skin diseases and sores had ravaged their bodies, and the few brown teeth that remained were rotting in their mouths. They stood scratching their heads, which were crawling with lice, and staring curiously out of eyes blotched with yellow matter and dirt as if they had not washed for months. The worst features of all were the huge lumps under their chins. Their ugliness repulsed me and I closed my eyes whispering, 'Lord, how can I love these people? I feel so sick just to look at them. How can I love them?'

I walked over to a water pump to be alone with Jesus for a moment and sort out my churning emotions. Suddenly, the Spirit of the Lord came upon me in just the same way as He did when the Lord gave me His call to the Philippines. He lifted me above the grotesque scene and I seemed to experience Ezekiel's vision:

> The hand of the LORD was upon me, and He brought me out by the Spirit of the LORD, and set me in the middle of a valley; it was full of bones. He led me to and fro among them, and I saw a great many bones on the floor of the valley, bones that were very dry. He asked me, 'Son of man, can these bones live?' I said, 'O Sovereign LORD, you alone know.' Then He said to me, 'Prophecy to these bones and say to them: "Dry bones, hear the Word of the LORD! This is what the Sovereign LORD says to these bones: I will make breath enter you and you will come to life. I will attach tendons to you and make flesh come upon you... and you will come to life. Then you will know that I am the LORD" (Ezek. 37:1-6).

I became aware that I was still standing by the water pump, and had been crying out to the Lord in tongues with tears rolling down my cheeks. I saw that these people were indeed the dry bones in the valley, without hope or life, dead through the weight of their sin. But although the wages of sin are death, the gift of God is eternal life through Christ Jesus, and I knew that in those moments in the spirit, He had promised to recreate their lives, to replace their hearts of stone with hearts of flesh (Ezek. 36:26).

As the anointing of the Lord lifted, the instinctive repulsion began to return – but now I was able to see these people from God's perspective. I began to walk forward, stooping to pick up a little child and moving to embrace a woman. As I did so, the voice of the Lord came to me, 'I do not judge people by the colour of their skin, nor by their clothes, nor by anything in their outward appearance. I judge people by the motives of their heart and I love these people.'

Instantly the sense of repulsion left me. My heart was filled with a great love for these people, and I walked among them freely. I no longer cared about the lice and the skin diseases. I simply wanted them to know that Jesus loved them, that they were of value in God's sight. Because of the love that He had put in my heart for them, these primitive people came to accept me and love me in return, revealing a tenderness and warmth I could not have imagined.

They led Susan and me to a little bamboo hut which was to be our home for as long as we wanted. The men were welcomed to share the huts of families in the village. No furniture of any kind adorned this most humble of dwellings: the floor itself provided my table, chair and bed, but I was thankful merely for the shelter from the merciless sun. As our little party sat cross-legged on the floor, I asked the pastor how these people survived.

'With great difficulty,' he replied with a sad smile. 'Those terraces of rice paddies you saw provide their staple diet, though the bowls of rice they eat each day are even more tasteless than you would think because they have no salt! Those gruesome lumps on their necks are goitres due to the lack of iodine in their diet. They also grow coffee beans but they haven't the skill, the tools or the raw materials to cultivate any vegetables – and even if they did, the soil is so poor that little would grow. In the height of the dry season, the ground is so parched and hard that no plant or vegetable can live. The only ploughing is in the rice paddies where a thin, decrepit caribou is shared by the whole village to turn over the soil. Some of the richer families have one pig, and on very special occasions it is killed, but it is difficult and costly to replace. Otherwise, their only meat is snake or wild dog, quite a luxury!'

When we had rested a little, we emerged from the tiny hut and found that the natives had prepared a meal for us, not surprisingly rice and coffee. The greyish morass of hot, sticky rice had absolutely no taste and very little texture, but it took away the hunger pains gnawing at my stomach. With my hunger appeased, my next task was to find out where the nearest water was. I was rather taken aback to discover it was an hour's hike away and that the river bed was nearly dried up. Instead I drew a cupful of water from the drinking pump and carefully washed my face and hands. Oh for a warm deep bath – with bubbles! I sighed ruefully, and then laughed as I reflected that these natives would have no idea what a bath even looked like, and would behold me with awe and wonder if I emerged from a cloud of bubbles!

Darkness was descending like a blanket over the Stone Age community carved out of the mountainside, and the night air came alive with strange calls and eerie cries. Cicadas droned like aeroplanes above our heads and the occasional rustle of leaves suggested that larger creatures were watching our camp. Once or twice a pair of yellow eyes glinted for a moment in the dying fire then disappeared into the blackness. Everyone was preparing for sleep, and I was handed a rush mat for a bed. Tiny bugs, spiders and insects crawled among the webbing, but I knew that someone had generously given it up and I accepted it gratefully. After pulling across the piece of bamboo that formed the door of the hut, I lay down wearily on the mat, and with a few words of prayer, I found myself drifting swiftly to sleep.

A few hours later, I was woken by the bright shafts of moonlight streaming through the open square cut out of the bamboo wall which formed a 'window'. My bones were aching from lying on the hard bamboo floor, and I lay listening to the mournful sound of wild dogs hunting in the distance, then, more ominous still, the insidious beat of tribal drums high up in the mountains where the most savage of the Bute Bute lived. A cold sweat pricked my skin and I shivered in the humid night air, noticing suddenly the weird shadows that lurked in the corner of my lonely hut. Fear began to crawl across my scalp as I imagined a stealthy figure climbing through the window with a long knife to claim the supreme trophy – a white head. Never in my life had I been gripped by such fear. My impulse was to leap up and run, yet my legs seemed paralysed with fright.

Panic seized me as I realised that I had nowhere to run to, half-way up a remote mountain with no clear path to lead me to civilisation and safety. All I could do was pray in tongues, and as the heavenly words pierced the darkness, I once more found myself commanding the spirit of fear to leave in the name of Jesus. Then I asked the Lord to send me four angels, two to stand at my head and two to stand at my feet, and while I praised Him for His power and provision, I felt His touch irradiate my whole body with peace, and all traces of fear leave. The sense of His angelic bodyguard was almost a tangible presence in the hut, and I closed my eyes in complete security and trust. Never again did I feel fear like that. Every night for the remainder of my stay, I asked my Father for these four angels to guard over me while I slept. Hallelujah! He is faithful to His promises.

Morning burst through the window and I awoke to the sound of natives chattering and calling as the day's work commenced. I rolled up my mat and went out to the water pump to wash my face. Every child from the village gathered to watch the great event. The moment I emerged from the hut, they surged forward and followed me to the pump where they stared in amazement as I cleaned my teeth. When the toothpaste foamed round my mouth, they laughed and giggled, and I made funny grimaces at them using the foam to make my face like a clown's. The dark little urchins roared with laughter, and a bond of friendship and confidence was forged already.

I soon realised the repetitive monotony of this primitive life, the great cycle of birth and death bringing little change in the impoverished life styles and the expectations of each generation. Day after day, from dawn till dusk, they toiled in the paddy fields for a bowl of sticky rice, the men chained to the wheel of unending labour, the women sentenced to almost continual childbearing, until the health and strength of both were broken.

Every girl or woman above the age of puberty was pregnant and suckled another child, trailing behind her

88

anything up to ten others. The mothers carried their suckling children in a sling, sometimes on their backs, sometimes across their chests for breast feeding, unselfconscious of this or their own nakedness as they were of all their bodily functions, having no sense of hygiene. They must have thought I was extraordinary, covering my body with clothes in the unbearable heat, and wandering in the mountains instead of caring for husband and children and stirring the pot of rice.

It was arranged that we would have a meeting that evening, and I spent most of the day in my hut, avoiding the overpowering sunlight and studying the Word of God every moment I had. I looked to the Holy Spirit to teach me, trusting in the Lord's promise that, 'When He, the Spirit of truth, comes, He will guide you into all truth. He will not speak on His own; He will speak only what He hears, and He will tell you what is yet to come' (John 16:13).

How good that we are not dependent on human knowledge and teaching. In that remote mountain village, the Lord God Himself interpreted the Scriptures to me by His Spirit, and led me into a deeper understanding of His character and purposes. If there was anything I could not understand, I would pray to my Father and the Holy Spirit would always bring the answer to my mind and spirit.

The heat of midday bore down upon us. The villagers sank to the ground in the shade, overcome by the throbbing brilliance of the sun and blistering temperature. All the village suddenly fell silent and even the birds and insects seemed unable to sing or move in the suffocating heat. I, too, fell asleep, and in the quietness of that time, the Lord gave me the message to preach to the people that evening. When I awoke, my mind was full of His words and I sat up to write what He had given me:

[Jesus said] 'Unless a man is born again, he cannot see the kingdom of God.' 'How can a man be born when he is old?' Nicodemus asked. 'Surely he cannot enter a second time into his mother's womb to be born?' Jesus answered . . . 'Unless a man is born of water and the Spirit he cannot enter the kingdom of God' (John 3:3-5).

When you are delivered from your mother's womb, you are born of flesh; the second birth is the birth of the spirit. You must be born of water and of the spirit to enter the kingdom of heaven, to receive the abundant life that lasts forever and forgiveness for your wickedness and evil deeds. We all have sin within us, for, 'If we claim to be without sin, we deceive ourselves and the truth is not in us' (1 John 1:8). God is pure and holy. He wants His people to be holy too, so He made a law that sin must be punished: 'The wages of sin is death' (Rom. 6:23). 'Unless you repent, you . . . will all perish' (Luke 13:3). But He is also faithful and just, and in His great love the Lord sent His beloved Son to pay the penalty for, our sin: ' . . . but the gift of God is eternal life' (Rom. 6:23).

'For God so loved the world that He gave His one and only Son, that whoever believes in Him shall not perish but have eternal life' (John 3:16). God promised that whoever turned from their wicked ways and believed in Jesus as their Saviour would be born again and have eternal life:

> To all who recieved Him, to those who believed in His name, He gave the right to become the children of God – children born not of natural descent, nor of human decision or a husband's will, but born of God (John 1:12-13).

> . . . if you confess with your mouth, 'Jesus is Lord', and believe in your heart that God raised Him from the dead, you will be saved. For it is with your heart that you believe and are justified, and it is with your mouth that you confess and are saved (Rom. 10:9-10).

To be born again, you must ask the Lord Jesus to forgive you of your sin and then ask Him to come and live in your heart by His Holy Spirit. Your sins are washed away since He took the punishment for them by shedding His own blood on a Cross. He paid the penalty for all our wrongdoing, for it was God's law that the wages of sin were death, then He rose from the dead so that we could share His eternal life. The Holy Spirit then joins Himself to your spirit, bringing this wonderful gift of eternal life.

Your lifestyle begins to change. Once the character of the devil was in your heart – hatred, jealousy, anger, criticism, lust; now the Holy Spirit lives inside you, and you are no longer bound to these things. You become a new creation, recreated in the image of God with His perfect nature, and are filled with love, joy, peace, patience, kindness, goodness, faithfulness, gentleness, self-control. But, to experience these things, you need to renew your mind, washing and cleansing it by the reading of God's Word, the Holy Bible, which tells us how we should live our lives. 'Let us draw near to God with a sincere heart in full assurance of faith, having our hearts sprinkled to cleanse us from a guilty conscience and having our bodies washed with pure water' (Heb. 10:22). In that way, you will understand and receive more of your Father's great love for you, and will long to serve Him and do His will, free from all bondage and full of the power of His mighty Holy Spirit.

Every native from the village attended the service that evening. The pastor taught them some gospel choruses and preached a little about the meaning of these songs and why we should praise and worship our God. Then it was my turn to speak and every word was interpreted so that the villagers heard the message of God's love in a language and context they could understand.

Powerfully, silently, the Holy Spirit began to breathe upon these dry bones lying in their spiritual death, convicting them of their sins and need of God's life. Repent, repent. Unless you repent, you shall all perish. The entire village got on its knees and asked the Lord Jesus to forgive them and lead them into life. As they did so, the Spirit of the one true God fell upon that tiny mountain community as if these primitive people commanded His sole attention and love. But His ways are mighty and mysterious, and it is difficult to describe what happened next, except that with the great Creator, salvation means *wholeness*, bringing healing, restoration and order to mind, body and spirit.

I walked over to one of the women whose neck was bloated and distorted by one of the hideous goitres, a lump bigger than a tennis ball. I laid my right hand on the huge growth, raised my other to the almighty Lord of heaven and earth, and began to pray in the Spirit. I had no idea of what was going to happen for I had gone over to this woman simply in obedience to the Holy Spirit. Suddenly I felt the lump begin to dissolve and shrink, melting under my hand. I opened my eyes and stared in disbelief at the woman's neck, filled with incredulity as my human understanding struggled to grasp the situation. In that split second of doubting, the goitre grew back to its original size! I was overcome with emotion, full of remorse at my lack of faith, and I cried out to the Lord to forgive my doubt. I placed my hand on the growth for the second time, and instantly the goitre disappeared! Wonder filled us all as we witnessed the miraculous power of God, though I had also seen how doubt and unbelief could rob a person of his healing and thwart the Lord in his fulfilment of His purposes.

The natives had no doubts about the reality and love of their new Saviour now. They all wanted me to pray for them. The power that raised Jesus from the dead began to move among them and, as the Holy Spirit came upon them, they could not stand, but fell backwards to the ground. When He was on the earth, Jesus healed all those who came to Him. Now He only seeks a channel, an openness to His touch. Fevers, skin diseases, goitres, pain, all were disappearing instantly before our eyes. I had never seen the love and power of God at work so gloriously. All around me, these simple villagers were receiving the gift of tongues too, praising and worshipping their new-found Lord with joy and adoration.

Out of the crowd, a little boy came hobbling towards me, crippled by some malformation in his legs. His eyes looked up at me hopefully. Could this great God make him walk properly? I sat him down and took his two little feet in my hands. One leg was stunted and withered, inches shorter than the other good leg. As I prayed in the Spirit, the crippled leg actually grew down, straightening and strengthening until both heels met. Leaping up, he stared at his new leg in round-eyed astonishment, then in three bounds he was gone, shouting at the top of his voice with excitement and glee.

As for me, the realisation of what was happening made me

sink to my knees as I tried to come to terms with the limitlessness of God's ability, and the vastness of His care and mercy. Nothing is impossible with God. The dry bones the Lord had shown me were no longer dead, but born again of the Holy Spirit, made alive by His breath, the same power that filled the crucified body of the Lord Jesus, and raised Him in a glorious, immortal body to live and reign for ever. Because He lives, we live too, abiding in Him and sharing in His abundance whatever our circumstances. There was now no fear and condemnation for the mountain people who hitherto had been ruled by superstition and anxiety. Even death, an ever-present threat, was swallowed up in victory, for they saw it was the door through which they could begin a conscious life in the presence of this gracious God of love.

He always brings to completion a work He has begun (Phil. 1:6). This was our comfort as we said goodbye to the transformed people of this mountain village. God had replaced their hearts of stone with hearts of flesh, and we knew that we could trust them to a faithful Creator who would feed and guide them into a deeper knowledge of Him. They began to build a bamboo church, and on the morning of our departure everyone met there at five thirty to commit each other to the Lord's care. It was arranged that the village chief and two of his flock should go to the Miracle Bible College for three years to learn the Word of God, and then come back to teach their people. The chief stepped forward and shook hands with me lovingly, explaining that each family had given a handful of rice and some coffee beans with a few white beans as a love gift to me. I was deeply moved, for I knew the sacrifice that this gift would mean, that they were denying themselves to express their love and appreciation for what they had received. To accept this gift would mean taking the food from their very mouths, yet to refuse it would be a rejection of their trust and friendship. All around, a silent circle of faces watched anxiously, hopefully, waiting to see how I would react. With gladness and gratitude, I welcomed the gift, and the uncertain expressions changed to grins of satisfaction. I shall never forget the joy which shone on their faces as each family came and placed a

93

handful of rice and a few coffee beans mingled with white on a piece of old rush mat. Then came the warm embraces, and we were gone.

Struggling back through the rice paddies, I reflected on the bond that God had forged between us since bringing me to see them from His perspective, with His eyes of compassion – God's beautiful children. And just as Jesus caught none of the diseases of the people with whom He mixed, so not even a head-louse had afflicted me, and I had remained unharmed by the poisonous waters in which the higher mountain tribes washed their disease-ridden bodies.

> Surely He will save you . . . from the deadly pestilence. He will cover you with His feathers, and under His wings you will find refuge; His faithfulness will be your shield and rampart. You will not fear the terror of night, nor the arrow that flies by day, nor the pestilence that stalks in the darkness, nor the plague that destroys at midday. If you make the Most High your dwelling – even the Lord who is my refuge – then no harm will befall you, no disaster will come near your tent. For He will command His angels concerning you to guard you in all your ways; they will lift you up in their hands, so that you will not strike your foot against a stone. You will tread upon the lion and the cobra; you will trample the great lion and the serpent (Psa. 91:3-13).

## Chapter Fifteen

The Lord's eyes run to and fro about the earth, searching for His lost sheep. No forest, valley or ocean is too deep for His gaze to penetrate and His love to pierce. His sight had rested on a place called Lewan, buried deep in the jungle, and it was here that His Spirit next led me to share His gift of love and hope.

No roads could push through the dense undergrowth, so we had to hike once more through the rice paddies and then cut a way through the tangled depths of the jungle paths. Trees of every size, shape and colour rose on all sides, and from the shadows of their foliage, brightly coloured birds darted with startled cries. Many branches were bent low with their burdens of ripe fruit – bananas, mangoes and all kinds of exotic fruits. Richness and abundance characterised this lush green world, in marked contrast to the poverty we had just left. The ground teemed with insect life, a writhing, swarming carpet of weird, many-legged creatures, beetles, lizards, snakes, mosquitoes and spiders the size of my hand. Occasionally a monkey swung lithely through the trees and chattered to us from a distance, knowing that too much curiosity would find him in the cooking pot.

The hike was long and arduous, but eventually we arrived safely at a little village where a number of inhabitants were Christians and greeted us with the warmth of long-lost brothers and sisters. A Filipino woman led this tiny flock, a beautiful handmaiden of the Lord, and under her prayer and faith a tremendous sense of the peace of God now reigned in that remote mountain settlement, deep in the jungle. The beauty of His holiness hung in the rich foliage of the trees and breathed through the golden twilight air. A second Garden of Eden it seemed, and I found refreshment and rest during our days of ministry there.

Evening was the time I loved best. As the last fingers of sunlight trailed scarlet threads on the distant mountain tops, and dusk drew itself like a veil across the face of the earth, I would make my way to a spring which cascaded down the mountainside and was channelled along a piece of hollowed bamboo to burst in a shower of cool silver drops over a glittering pool. Here this earthy paradise produced a spectacle more lovely than all imagining, for hosts of fireflies would gather in the shades of twilight and illuminate the pool with a thousand glowing lights, settling on the trees and transforming the scene into a Christmas picture.

Meetings were held every evening in the little village church and from far and wide natives from the surrounding tribes came to hear the white woman preach. But she simply gave way to the Holy Spirit for He was there in power to heal and save all who turned to the Lord. The kingdom of God welcomed many new children during those days, and pain, fevers, diseases and infirmities were all instantly banished in the name of Jesus Christ. One little boy of seven had been stone deaf from birth, and after prayer I placed my watch against his ear. With a look of incredulity, he softly made the sound, 'tick tick tick tick', God having loosed his tongue as well as his ears. When He was on the earth, the Lord Jesus loved in practice, not just in theory, meeting people's needs and bringing wholeness to their bodies as well as their spirits. He is no different today, and God was showing these people in this isolated place His love and greatness through miracles.

We went family visiting on several occasions, hiking long distances through the jungle in temperatures of over a hundred degrees, so that we could only reach a couple of homes each day. Choruses of praise and thanksgiving encouraged our steps as the perspiration coursed down our backs, but we knew that our strength lay in the joy of the Lord. And our joy was great, for at every turn souls were saved and bodies healed as God hourly confirmed His Word with signs following.

On the return journey from one of these family visits, we

came upon a small river whose cool green depths were an irresistible temptation to our weary limbs. The idea of immersing my whole body in clean, cold water surged to my mind like a long-forgotten dream, and in a second I had plunged fully clothed into the gentle flow. It had been months since I had even seen so much water, and actually to submerge myself under it seemed a delicious luxury. The whole party splashed about recklessly like children at the seaside, but soon we had to drag ourselves reluctantly from the refreshing waters as night was approaching and we were still some distance from the village. As I stretched out a hand to grasp a rock in order to pull myself up, a sharp pain shot through the flesh of my third finger and I jerked my hand away swiftly to see blood pouring from a deep cut. The festering wounds I had seen among the natives made me imagine in a flash the consequences of such a cut. Without antiseptic or bandages, the wound would surely become infected and cause much pain and trouble. The river swirled round my waist as I stood and stared at the blood gushing from the open cut, engrained with dirt and grit from the rock. Panic began to rise within me. Then, in an instant, I recognised the author of this fear, and I took hold of the authority that I had learnt would release the power of the risen Lord in every situation.

'Satan, you're a liar!' I rebuked him sternly then, turning to God, I prayed, 'My Father in heaven, in the name of Jesus, I ask you to draw the flesh together and heal this cut. Thank you, Lord.'

I swished my hand in the water to get rid of the dirt and then looked at the finger. The wound had closed, and there was no sign of blood, only a hairline mark could be traced where the flesh had joined together. The God who created woman by taking a rib from the side of Adam and closing the flesh was well able to perform such elementary healing and it was instantaneous and complete. Whether great or small, all things are in His hands.

# Chapter Sixteen

Once again the Lord was moving me on. At the last meeting, He laid it on my heart to tell the people that Jesus was coming back soon and to warn them against taking the mark of the Beast (Rev. 13:16-17; 14:9-10). Then it was back to the jungle track to begin the long journey to Sanfernando to attend the graduation of the Bible students at Miracle Mission.

We left the village at three thirty in the morning for the hike through the jungle would take nearly four hours and we had to reach the highway to catch a jeep by seven thirty. It was an eerie experience, stumbling along mountain tracks, wading through murky rivers in almost pitch blackness, surrounded by strange calls and sudden rustles behind us in the dense undergrowth. Flickering dimly in front was the faint light of the guide's kerosine lamp carried high on his shoulder, and ever so often his sharp call would cut through the still, dark air, warning of some danger near by. In a wonderful way, God guided our footsteps, protected our bodies and encouraged our hearts – but I was still relieved when He rolled back the curtain of darkness to reveal the morning light!

Eventually the long march ended as we climbed on to the roadside and I was left alone to await the jeep. When it finally appeared I could hardly believe my eyes. People and baggage were crowded on the roof, clinging to the bonnet, hanging on to the back rail so that the jeep seemed submerged under a sea of bodies. I wondered rather hopelessly how there could possibly be enough room for me but, as the driver stopped, one of the natives promptly offered me his seat while he calmly latched himself on to the vehicle by just one foot and hand. Others adopted this precarious position around the jeep, and somehow it managed to stagger on its way, groaning and creaking under the massive load. I don't know if any fell by the wayside, but good spirits were maintained on the incredible journey, and at last we came to a market town, the destination of many of the mountain people. For the next three hours, the journey was less cramped, though the driver, overjoyed at the lighter weight and manoeuvrability of the vehicle, drove like a madman along the treacherous mountain tracks. By this time, however, I was getting used to this cavalier style of driving and was able to sit back and enjoy the spectacular views of the mountains stretching endlessly on to the sea.

By nightfall, we were still far from Sanfernando and the jeep stopped overnight at a town called Tigigerough. I was taken to a home in the town centre where a wealthy and influential family, who had some command of the English language, kindly offered me shelter for the night. On arriving, I discovered that the family was having some kind of celebration, and they explained that exactly one year ago to the day, the eldest son had died. Apparently, it was their custom that the widow should remain in mourning for one year after the husband's death, and when the time was fulfilled she was free to marry again.

On this night, candles burned in every room, and the whole family were bowing down before idols, praying for the spirit of the dead son. The strange atmosphere was disturbing, and their bondage to these pagan rituals made me concerned and uncomfortable, but I was loath to repay their kindness by disrupting a family ceremony – besides, I had nowhere else to go in that strange town.

I sought out the lady of the house and explained that I was exhausted after travelling since before dawn and could she show me where I was to sleep. As she opened the door on a small room I was glad to see a bed in it, but then my eye rested on the bizarre sight of a table completely laden with food, set with one place already filled with delicacies. Next to a bottle of wine was one glass, half full, and beside that a candle flickered and waved. On the wall behind the table stood twelve weird statues ranged on shelves, and near by a large picture of a long-haired, bearded young man with melancholy eyes. I stood rooted to the spot. Surely she did not expect me to eat all this food tonight? Catching sight of my startled look, the hostess began to explain in her broken English that the meal was to feed the spirit of the dead son which would come in the night to consume what it needed. She told me not to blow the candle out, but to allow it to burn all night. Then she walked out and left me standing there, stunned into silence. I could sense evil all around me.

'I can't stay here,' I muttered to myself, as I felt the glassy eyes of the statues boring into me. But as I turned to hurry from the macabre scene, a tremendous peal of thunder crashed through the heavens followed by a brilliant flash of lightning. Instantly the rain beat upon the house like gunfire, and I realised that escape was impossible for I should be drenched to the skin in seconds and should never be able to find shelter; I should have to remain in that room all night. As the thunder pealed again and the lightning illuminated the ghostly meal and threw distorted shadows of the hideous statues on the walls, I found myself in the grip of paralysing fear. Reaching out to the Lord, I began to pray, 'He who lives in me is stronger than he who lives in the world. The Holy Spirit within me is stronger than the devil who is in the world.'

Claiming these promises firmly in the name of Jesus, I lay down on the bed, which to my surprise was soft and comfortable, and clutching my Bible to my chest I asked the Lord to protect me while I slept. At once the peace of God came upon me, soothing my aching body and calming my pounding heart. I fell into a sound sleep.

When I awoke the following morning, the food was still on the table, surveyed balefully by the twelve statues and the sad young man. I got up and blew the candle out, then went outside to the water pump to wash. When I returned to the room, all the food had disappeared. I opened my Bible at random and read, 'Thou shalt have no other gods before me. Thou shalt not make unto thee any graven images. Thou shalt not bow down thyself to them.' I knew that this was the message God wanted to give the family.

Armed with my Bible, I went to find my hostess and discovered the whole family seated at the table eating breakfast. My heart sank when I saw that they were eating the food that had been offered to the spirit of the dead son. I could eat nothing, but instead opened my Bible, and began to read the portion of Scripture that God had given me. A chair scraped sharply as the lady of the house rose abruptly and walked out, but her husband remained and listened attentively as I shared the mighty miracles that God had performed up in the mountains, and testified to the power of the one true God, the risen Lord Jesus Christ. Tears filled his eyes as the message of eternal life touched his heart, and I prayed with him to be born again into the family of God. I left him with the promise on his lips that he would read the Word of God, and I knew that the seed which had been planted would be fed by the Holy Spirit and bear fruit in the life of the whole family.

## Chapter Seventeen

Miracle Mission was buzzing with activity and excitement. Children from the orphanage ran out to tell me that 'Papa' Shields was back home, and I soon discovered the reason for the rejoicing. Some months ago, Revd. Shields, an American missionary who had settled in the Philippines to work for the Lord through the Mission, had experienced a massive heart attack. Only fifteen per cent of his heart remained functioning, and doctors had not expected him to live, or at best they thought he would have an invalid's existence, and he had been sent home to America to die.

In the meeting that evening, the hall resounded to cries of 'Praise the Lord' as Revd. Shields rose to address the congregation. Few knew that he had arrived back in the Philippines and great gasps could be heard as they looked up and saw him, for word had gone round that he would never recover far less return to the Mission. Joy and wonder glowed on their faces as they thanked the Lord Jesus for sending their beloved Papa Shields back home to them. As he began to preach, the anointing of God fell upon him and he delivered an inspired message of God's saving grace and power which gave vision to the graduates going out into the world to serve Him. It was a memorable evening and well worth the long, difficult journey from the mountain provinces.

But a double blessing was in store. The Sunday service in the chapel the following morning witnessed one of the most remarkable experiences of my life. The chapel was filled to overflowing, the aisles were packed, the benches placed in the front yard were all crammed with expectant faces, and people stood all around. Every heart was lifted with abandon to praise and worship the Lord Jesus, and the mighty presence of God enveloped the small chapel and the crowd outside. As I worshipped with all my heart the God who had worked such wonders and revealed so clearly His wealth of love and healing power, the Holy Spirit began to move upon me so that I shook uncontrollably and found myself speaking in tongues with a fluency and exaltation I had never known. It seemed that I was no longer in the church surrounded by people. Instead, a brilliant golden light bathed me from head to foot, hiding me from the outside world in a cloud of glory.

Suddenly, for the first time in my life, I heard the *audible* voice of God. Clear, strong, authoritative, the words came distinctly to my ears, 'BE HEALED IN THE NAME OF JESUS.' Astounded, I looked to the front of the chapel and at that moment Revd. Shields said, 'If there is anyone in the congregation who is sick, please stand.' As many people rose, I stepped forward and again the mighty voice of God spoke to my ears, 'BE HEALED IN THE NAME OF JESUS.' Raising my hand over the congregation, I repeated God's words – and instantly everyone with any pain or disease was healed. I was dumbfounded. But God is committed to His Word, and as His command rang through the air, the healing power of Jesus swept through the church, making whole all that was broken without further human intervention or prayer. Some people were crying, others were laughing, some were shaking as God ministered to their spirits as well as their bodies, while others had dropped to the floor as His touch came upon them. Thanksgiving brought even greater joy and the more we praised and worshipped our glorious Lord, the more He poured out His Spirit and love upon us. The blessings He rained upon us that evening were permanent and real, leading many into a deeper knowledge of Him and expectation of His ability to do through them even greater works than Jesus did.

Two weeks were spent in sweet fellowship with God's children from both the Philippines and the United States. I believe I had a glimpse of what heaven will be like.

# Chapter Eighteen

It was time for my American brothers and sisters to return to their own country and, as the Mission settled down to a normal routine after the fortnight's festivities, I began to feel God calling me back to the interior of the island. I had been invited by a Revd. Calamoing to minister in his area and it seemed that now was the Lord's time. As I sought the Lord, He confirmed that I should leave the coming Monday. Meanwhile, there was work to be done. The following morning I was to minister in the prison at Sanfernando – with Mother Mabel.

Miracle Mission was proud and fond of its oldest member. Mother Mabel was in her eighties and had been serving God in the Philippines most of her life. She had a special burden for the prison in Sanfernando where she had sown many seeds of faithful, earnest prayer, but so far only a meagre harvest had been reaped from the sin-hardened institution. Her deepest longing was to see revival come to that place and, ever trusting in God's graciousness and inscrutable ways, she had asked me to share the Lord there before I left.

We didn't look that convincing or mighty a deputation as we assembled outside the prison gates at eight thirty that morning – little Mother Mabel, her diminutive figure lit by the bright blue eyes which shone out of her nut-brown face, three young students from the Mission, and myself.

The guards unlocked the heavy steel doors to reveal the prisoners herded like cattle into the gaunt community room. A hollow bang echoed down the corridors as the guards went out, locking and bolting the massive door, leaving us alone with 130 sullen-looking men.

The prison housed men guilty of every kind of crime – murder, rape, theft, arson – and they were crowded together indiscriminately, hardened criminals with young boys, the mentally insane with the sound-minded, but all had a wild, desperate look on their faces. The room stank, waves of foul smell floating on the stifling, humid air, barely relieved by any ventilation. The men were all talking among themselves, and seemed so uninterested in our presence that I began to wonder if I had made a mistake in believing God had told me to come here. I turned to Him and prayed, 'Father, in the name of Jesus, let your anointing fall on me so that I can get your message through to these men.'

Then I raised my voice boldly above the din and shouted, 'I don't have to be here, you know, and unless you sit down, shut up and listen, I'm not prepared to waste any more time on you!'

The effect was dramatic. A startled silence fell upon them, and they sat down meekly on the floor like schoolchildren, staring curiously at the strange white woman. I had their undivided attention but, in the expectant hush, my mind went a complete blank. I closed my eyes and said simply, 'Help me, Jesus' then I opened my mouth in faith and began to preach. It was my voice doing the speaking, it was me who walked in among the prisoners, but the message was straight from the throne of God. There was no interpreter. I cannot recall what I said to those men, for what came out of my mouth was not from my own mind or understanding. I do not even know if I was speaking English or some language they understood, but I remember moving through the crowd, laying my hands upon them, and at one point saying something about angels. Gradually the expressions of resentment, and despair faded, and tears welled up in the eyes of these hard, embittered men, soon coursing down their cheeks as their hearts were melted by Jesus's love. Struggling awkwardly to their knees, they began to reprent of their sin and, with me leading them in a prayer of repentance, they asked Jesus to come into their hearts and grant them eternal life.

Standing in the centre of that grim prison room, I found myself saying, 'Jesus is here with us now and wants to fill you with His Holy Spirit. He wants to give you the gift of tongues so that you can pray in a new heavenly language. All you have to do is come forward and receive.'

One man stepped forward and I placed my hand on his forehead and prayed that the Lord would fill him with His Spirit and give him the gift of tongues. Once more, the power of God reached down so that the man could not stand. He fell flat on his back, and as he lay there he began to praise God in a new language. I would not have imagined the voice of a criminal could sound so beautiful. One by one the prisoners came forward to receive this spiritual baptism, and each time I laid my hand on their forehead, they fell straight to the ground and praised God in tongues. Suddenly I felt a hand pulling on my sleeve, and looking round I saw a rough, unshaven face, streaked with dust and tears, looking suddenly young and vulnerable in its childlike excitement.

'I want Jesus to touch me again. Please pray for me once more.' Again I laid my hand on his head and prayed, 'Father, he wants a double portion!' And down he went again to the floor as the Spirit poured into his life.

I stood back and looked round. The stark prison hall was strewn with men lying on their backs praising God in different languages which only He could understand. Behind me, I caught sight of the guards with guns in their hands, staring through the grill of the steel doors with expressions of utter bewilderment. Blotting the sight out of my mind, I turned back and continued to pray for the prisoners as God led me, for He knew their needs, whether physical, spiritual or psychological, and wanted to bring the fullness of His kingdom into their resurrected lives. Mother Mabel flitted from prisoner to prisoner like an excited bird, radiant with joy as she prayed and talked with them. Every single prisoner received an individual touch from God, and when we said goodbye I knew that the prison would never be the same again. The work of the Holy Spirit would continue acording to God's progressive, creative plan, and I was sure that many prisoners who entered those gates might find not a sentence but a new hope and purpose, emerging saved, healed and forgiven.

## Chapter Nineteen

It was the familiar dawn that witnessed my departure for Dagupan, the Mission and Bible college to which I had been invited. Pastor Bonafacio Calamoing and his lovely Filipino wife ran a small mission in this remote area where the dialect of the surrounding tribes was particularly difficult, and evangelists had to learn the language before going to the outlying villages. Local people from that area who received Jesus as their Saviour often spent some time in the college being taught more about the Lord so that they could take the Word back to their homes. About twenty students, four teachers and the pastor and his wife lived in the community completely by faith, displaying a dedication to the Lord in an area where it would seem impossible for Him to support them.

I travelled by bus to Bagio City where another bus was waiting to carry me to my destination. I arrived at about eight o'clock in the evening, full of the joy of the Lord as I had a strong expectation that God was going to do great things during my time there. I soon found that He had gone before me, for I received the warmest welcome and immediately felt part of the family. The pastor and his wife insisted on giving up their bed for me as it was the only soft bed on the campus – a love gift from an American missionary – everyone else sleeping on hard bamboo. The same bamboo formed the walls of my room, carefully interleaved in a criss-cross pattern, and a bamboo lean-to screen made up the door. The ceiling was lined with strips of cardboard made from old boxes, and the floor was earthen, God's own ground. The 'bathroom' was a makeshift bamboo erection containing simply a large zinc basin, but at least I did not have to go to the river each morning for water as students carried it up in pails every day from the one water pump, half a mile away, which served the whole village. As for the lavatory, I shared it with a pig who lived there permanently and who was mildly surprised at the interruptions, though I struck up quite a friendship with it towards the end. Food in this region consisted mainly of fish and the inevitable rice, fish providing the main source of the people's income since they farmed fish, breeding them in huge pans.

The following weeks were spent ministering to the Bible students and preaching the gospel in the neighbouring villages. On one occasion I stood before the Bible class and opened the Word at 1 Corinthians 2 verses 1-5:

> When I came to you, brothers, I did not come with eloquence or superior wisdom as I proclaimed to you the testimony about God. For I resolved to know nothing while I was with you except Jesus Christ and Him crucified. I came to you in weakness and fear, and with much trembling. My message and my preaching were not with wise and persuasive words, but with a demonstration of the Spirit's power, so that your faith might not rest on men's wisdom, but on God's power.

I began to speak and once more the anointing of the Lord came upon me. Looking back, I wish that these meetings could have been recorded so that I could listen to some of the messages that the Holy Spirit preached through me. On this occasion, I was astounded at the words which came tumbling out of my mouth. The Lord was saying that we are living in the last days. God is going to demonstrate His power on this earth in a way that the world has never seen before nor even dreamt of. People will be translated by the Spirit of God in a moment of time and appear in different nations of the world. As these words poured out, I suddenly knew that I would be one of those chosen ones.

The Holy Spirit began to move among the students. One by one, they either fell to the ground flat on their backs or landed on their knees as the Lord ministered to the needs of the individuals. Some were healed, some were delivered, and nearly all were baptised in the Holy Spirit so that the place rang with the sound of their voices praising God in their new-found heavenly language.

When the meeting was ended, my mind was full of the knowledge that the Lord would translate me from place to place. I knelt and prayed, asking the Lord to give me confirmation in His Word. Immediately, God led me to Acts 8 verses 39-40:

When they came up out of the water, the Spirit of the Lord suddenly took Philip away, and the eunuch did not see him again, but went on his way rejoicing. Philip, however, appeared at Azotus and travelled about, preaching the gospel in all the towns until he reached Caesarea.

We then began to go and preach in the outlying villages. More and more I was convinced we were living in the last days. What we were seeing was the latter rain, God pouring out His Spirit upon all flesh, saving souls and healing bodies, establishing His kingdom of peace, wholeness and joy where the kingdom of darkness had reigned before.

One memorable miracle of that week was with a man who had suffered a stroke ten years previously and which had left one side of his face paralysed, grotesquely transforming his whole appearance. Children would run away from this monster-man, and even adults averted their eyes in embarrassment and horror. But when I prayed for him in the name of Jesus, the twisted features straightened as God healed the damaged brain and he became completely normal, able to speak and smile and praise His Saviour. Shouts of joy echoed through the rough native church as the villagers witnessed this miracle in their midst, and through the channel of their faith and praise, God was able to do many more wonders there.

The Lord then directed a small group of us to go to the tiny island of Pugaro, just off the coast. We forged our way over in a crude wooden boat, and within ten minutes of being on the island I began to feel desperately sick as though every ounce of energy had been drained from my body. My head swam and I thought I should collapse at any moment so I lay down in a hammock to try and concentrate my thoughts on

God. It was the pastor who suggested that the sickness might be a demonic attack by evil spirits, and he went on to explain that on this tiny island of only 150 people, five different cults ruled the inhabitants, dominating their lives with witchcraft, voodoo and spiritism.

As I lay in the hammock, feeling more ill every moment, I could sense the spiritual oppression in the heavy, uneasy atmosphere of the island, and all I wanted to do was get back in the boat and put it as far behind me as possible. Fighting down the nausea and dizziness, I suddenly recalled the words of Jesus in Luke 10 verse 19: 'I have given you authority to trample on snakes and scorpions and to overcome all the power of the enemy; nothing will harm you.' Dragging together my ebbing strength, I prayed, 'Satan, I will not accept any sickness you are trying to put on me. In the name of Jesus, I bind you and command you to be gone.'

I got up from the hammock, and instantly the sickness left me as the demons oppressing me were forced to flee at the mighty name of Jesus.

We walked around the island, inviting everyone to come and hear the gospel and see the power of God at work. I was followed all the time by a band of about thirty children, fascinated by the strange white colour of my skin. Darkness had fallen by the time the service began, and the only form of lighting was a single Tilly lamp hung from a nail above my head. We opened the meeting by singing praises to Jesus, but very soon the lamp began to sway about alarmingly and then went out, which seemed very strange as there was hardly a breath of wind. The service was halted while the lamp was relit and hung back on its nail, but within minutes it began to sway to and fro and quickly plunged us into pitch blackness once more.

The ritual was repeated, and this time I stood and opened my Bible to address the crowd of natives. I had not read more than six words when the lamp recommenced its wild antics and darkness reigned. Four times this happened in just fifteen minutes and on the last occasion, as I stood in the blackness while someone fumbled with the light, I began to get angry as I recognised that it was the devil who was trying

110

to disrupt the meeting. I stood there and again took authority over the usurper, 'Satan, I command you to leave these premises instantly in the name of Jesus!' My voice rang out through the dense night air, the flame burst into a bright, steady glow, and the meeting continued without any further interruption from the powers of darkness.

Nearly fifty people repented of their sins and asked Jesus to come into their lives, and then I called for anyone who needed healing in their physical body to come forward. Almost everyone surged forward at the same time and, as I stepped down from the wooden platform, the Holy Spirit began to move. Before I had a chance to lay hands on anyone, they all fell backwards as God Himself placed His hand upon them. Every single person that came forward was instantly and totally healed. One woman who had been completely paralysed down the whole of her right side, began to move her head, then raise her arm, then bend her knee, and finally dance with joy.

At the end of the service, one of the inhabitants of the island asked me if I would go with her to pray for her father who had been very ill for a long time. I was led by the light of the Tilly lamp through the island until we came to a little bamboo hut, and there I saw a tiny old man lying like an abandoned doll on the hard wooden floor. He was skin and bone and barely breathing, looking more dead than alive, and my heart was filled with compassion. He was too ill even to talk, and all I could do was kneel beside him, grasping his bony hand, and cry out to the Lord in tongues. I didn't know what to pray for a man so clearly on the very point of death, but I trusted that the Holy Spirit could reach down into his spirit and speak to him even as his earthly life was being extinguished.

I was then taken back to our little craft and we returned to the mainland by moonlight. The following day a message came from the island. Could the white woman go back as the old man had died? He was a well-known and respected old man, and a special funeral ceremony was to be arranged for him.

I was loath to return to that oppressed island, but we all

felt it was the Lord's will that we did, so we climbed into our fragile boat, just as huge, heavy drops of rain began to fall. Seconds later, great sheets of rain lashed us and we huddled together as the boat rolled dangerously through the angry sea. But the same Lord who rebuked the storm on Galilee gave protection to these disciples, and we reached dry land safely, our clothes drying on our backs within ten minutes of the rain's stopping.

I had never seen a dead body before, nor even attended a funeral, but I was requested to officiate at this one, the last ceremony for the revered old man. I could hardly refuse and reject this expression of trust, but it was with reluctance and hesitancy that I watched the body being placed in a rough bamboo coffin and carried to the funeral boat which would bear us to the graveyard back on the mainland. The crossing was nearly over when one of our group pointed out that all the pagan natives, the followers of the cults, who had refused to come to the meeting the previous night, would attend the funeral service and, sure enough, dozens of little black boats swarmed across the water behind us. The open coffin was laid out in the graveyard for everyone to see and, as the mourners filed past, the widow and daughter became hysterical and others soon took up their wailing cries.

Something had to be said to help these grief-stricken people, and aloud I called on the Lord for His help and inspiration. Once more the mantle of His anointing fell upon me in my weakness and need, just as it had done in the prison. All I can remember are the opening words, 'God has arranged this meeting. He has called you together today so that you might know the truth and the truth will set you free!' But after that, I had only a vague consciousness that God was sending out a beautiful message about the certainty of life after death, and before the end of the ceremony nearly all the heathen people had got on their knees and repented of their sins. I had not been able to imagine the benefit of returning to the island, but 'we know that all things work together for the good of those who love Him, who have been called according to His purpose' (Rom. 8:28), and I was certain that the old man had died in the will of God.

## Chapter Twenty

Every spare moment I had I spent studying the Word of God. The more I sought to know Him and understand His purposes, the more clearly He impressed on me the need to preach about the imminent return of the Lord Jesus and to warn about the rise of the Antichrist. It was not an easy topic to contemplate, far less preach, but if I tried to turn away from it, the Lord brought it forcibly back to my mind so that whenever I was not speaking of salvation and repentance, I preached about the signs of the last days and the urgency to be wise in the spirit and to prepare for the Lord's return. However, it was not difficult to see that the message was not received with enthusiasm or gladness, even by Christians, for everyone preferred to hear a gentle, easy message of God's love and goodwill towards men. I travelled round to a few more meetings in that area, but eventually the cold reception of my burden made me feel thoroughly discouraged, and I decided to shelve the message about the end-times, and just preach faith and love instead.

Only seventy pesos remained of my ready money and I needed to return to Sanfernando before I could draw any more cash. I left Dagupan with a promise that somehow in the future I would send money to help support the Bible students and teachers who worked and taught there for the sheer love of God and His kingdom.

When I arrived at Manila I got off the bus and discovered to my horror that I had disembarked at the wrong place. My first impulse was to get a taxi to the central bus station where I could catch a bus to Sanfernando, but when I looked in my purse I found only the seventy pesos, just enough for my bus fare home. As I stood there, quite helpless in this strange city, a man walked over to me, smiled, picked up my baggage, and walked off with it! An extraordinary peace came over me, and I quietly followed the tall figure for fifteen minutes, with never a word being spoken. Along numerous streets and through the market place he led me, until suddenly he halted, raised his hand and stopped an approaching jeep. He loaded in my baggage, helped me in, and then with another quiet smile he turned and disappeared into the jostling crowd. We travelled on through the streets of Manila until, to my amazement, the jeep came to a stop at the bus station opposite the stand for Sanfernando, and I was charged the equivalent of just a few pence for the ride. Praising God, I continued my journey safely, sure that the silent stranger was one of His angels sent to help me when I was lost and in need.

Miracle Mission was dear to my heart, and it was good to be back, getting almost knocked off my feet by the excited hugs of the little orphan children. I ran to greet Pastor Shields but was concerned to see that his face was sad. Quietly he explained that no one on the campus had eaten for two days as there was no money to buy rice. Straightaway, I went to the bank and drew enough money to keep everyone at the Mission fed for a few days. God had provided for all my needs, and to me it was simply a case of keeping open the channel of His supply. Next I learnt that the water and electricity bills had to be paid, so again I drew the cash to cover these needs, rejoicing as much as anyone at God's provision, for the money all belonged to Him and I just sought to use it as He directed.

As I was talking with Pastor Abbey a few days later, he mentioned their need of a jeep to take the students to the outlying districts to preach the gospel to the tribal peoples and mountain folk. I took that into my heart, and later that day my Father spoke to me, saying that there was enough money left from the sale of my house in England to buy the jeep, though I had no idea what sort of sum was required. To buy a new jeep would surely leave me penniless in a strange country, so I told the Lord that I would buy a second-hand jeep and reserve enough money to get back to England.

Immediately His voice spoke to my heart; 'Don't you trust

114

Me, Isabel?' I was filled with remorse and shame for I realised that I was prepared to trust the Lord as long as I had money in the bank and knew I had a safety rope to hold on to. This was the real test of my faith. Could I spend all my money on a new jeep and then trust God to supply my every need, relinquishing as I did so my ability to return to England? I thought of my family back home, and all that I loved about the British way of life, the countryside, the people, the comforts of Western society. Then I reflected on God's faithfulness during recent months, the miraculous way He had led me and cared for me, using me as the instrument of His saving power, and giving me the unmatchable joy of following in His will and knowing the assurance of His presence, provision and blessing. I had experienced His unreserved generosity, and in those few minutes I knew that to turn my back on this final call to obedience would mean an impoverished, unfulfilled existence thereafter. The battle was won. I resolved to buy the jeep for the Mission and immediately I saw how infinitely more valuable were the lost souls who would be saved through it than my earthly security. I rejoiced in God's perfect plan.

A dramatic turn of events halted any further activity for me. Within days of returning to the Mission, I was taken desperately ill, succumbing suddenly to a violent fever which carried me swiftly into delirium so that when I next awoke it was to find myself in a hospital bed. Through the haze of fever, I could see a green lizard darting crazily across the wall opposite me while insects and beetles danced a weird gavotte on the ceiling. I drifted back into unconsciousness and doctors gathered round my bed to diagnose the disease.

Typhoid fever was the verdict, a killer on many occasions, and even people who survived suffered severe illness for a long time. For days I was racked by the raging virus, delirious for much of the time, my very brain seeming to melt with the burning fever. Then chills would grip my body in a vice-like claw, and I would shake uncontrollably for hours so that every muscle in my body ached and seemed about to disintegrate. Revd. Shields and Pastor Abbey came to pray for me, but still the fever persisted unabated and the doctors began to lose hope. In my rare flashes of conscious understanding, I wondered why God had allowed the devil to put this awful disease on me, and I came to the conclusion that my work on this earth was finished. God had accomplished much and had enabled me to deliver to Him hundreds of souls who had received His salvation and healing. Soon I was to meet my Saviour, and I said my final prayers, expecting at any moment for the veil of flesh to be removed and to see Him face to face.

Suddenly my mind became curiously lucid and I was aware of lying in the bed, my body wasted by fever. I was alone, but an awesome presence seemed to fill the room and a sense of expectancy flooded through me. All at once, a clear, strong voice broke through the stifling air and came powerfully, unmistakably to my ears, 'YOU MUST GIVE THE MESSAGE TO THE CHURCH!' I held my breath and shivers of a different nature made my body tremble. Once more the authoritative voice of God resounded round the room, 'YOU MUST GIVE THE MESSAGE TO THE CHURCH!' At this point I did not understand what the message was, but not even the sun or moon could refuse to obey such an unequivocal command. I responded to Him with all my heart and a strong assurance came to me that soon the Lord would fully reveal His special plan for me. There was still work for me to do on this earth.

As I lay there, pondering on the mighty thing that had happened, an overwhelming desire for water suddenly swept over me and the fever began to wrap itself around me once more. I struggled out of bed and stumbled across the room, finding a shower in the corner. But as I turned the tap on, my weakened legs gave way and I collapsed on the floor with the water pouring over my body. Too feeble to move, I lay crumpled amid the rain of water, but instead of fear, great peace filled me, and I began to praise the Lord aloud: 'I love you, Jesus... Thank you, dear Lord... Praise you, Jesus...' The words tumbled out of my mouth and in those moments of sweet worship the fever just lifted from my body and all traces of the illness vanished instantly. I rose, dressed, and walked out of the hospital, leaving the doctors open-mouthed at the miraculous transformation.

In the next couple of days, I rejoiced in my new-found life and strength, expecting God's immediate direction, but no clearer word came concerning the message He had commanded me to preach. Meanwhile, a burning desire sprang up in my heart to visit the United States. I spent the entire day in prayer, seeking God as to whether it was His will, and the desire developed into an urgency. I decided to go into Manila and enquire about a visa, knowing the difficulty of obtaining such a thing at short notice. The simplicity and speed with which all the arrangements were made convinced me without doubt that this was God's leading. A further assurance came when Revd. Shields told me that he had been awarded a Doctor's degree in America, and needed someone to attend the approaching ceremony on his behalf. I left him with a cheque to cover the cost of the jeep, bought my ticket for Los Angeles and cashed a few extra dollars, which, to my knowledge, was all that remained of my money from the sale of my property. Now I was gloriously free, cast off from my earthly security, to be blown by the wind of the Spirit wherever God led.

## Chapter Twenty-One

Once again I was seated on an aeroplane, bound for another country; and once again I had no real knowledge of why I was going there. The plane landed at Los Angeles and all I had to do was find out the best means of transport to carry me to my destination, an address in the town of Des Moines given me by Revd Shields. Due to my total ignorance of the size of the United States and of all matters geographical generally, I was met with the shattering realisation that Des Moines was not just a few miles down the road, but over one thousand miles away! My heart sank, and my first thought was that I did not have enough money to pay my air fare there. But God had led me thus far. I went over to the counter, and asked for a ticket, in faith. Meanwhile, I opened my purse and began to count blindly, believing that my supply was from God. With only a handful of notes left, I approached the figure that was asked, then tears of joy began to run down my cheeks as the exact sum lay finally on the counter in front of me. I had to turn my face to hide my emotion from the girl, who was looking at me with concern. The Lord would not have left me stranded. In that moment of divine providence, I knew that I was in the perfect will of God. Only fourteen dollars remained, but with the King of heaven and earth, it was worth four thousand! I had no anxiety about anything.

I reached the address Revd Shields had given me and was received with warmth and hospitality by the good people there. The graduation ceremony was a few days away, so there was a little time to explore and speak to the people of God's goodness and work in the Philippines. On the first Sunday I visited the local 'church', Kingsway Cathedral. To my astonishment, a complete stranger walked over to me

118

and said, 'The Lord has laid it on my heart to bring this tape to church this morning, and He has just told me that you are the person I should give it to!'

I was intrigued to hear what was on it, and after the service I hurried back and switched it on. For the next hour I sat glued to the chair, hardly able to believe my ears. The exact same message I had been preaching in the Philippines about the rise of the Antichrist, the mark of the Beast, and the imminent return of the Lord Jesus, was recorded almost word for word on that tape, the same Scriptures, the same examples, the same MESSAGE! It all came flooding back. I remembered the day I decided not to preach that message any longer because it was not received with gladness. In that split second, I had walked out from under the umbrella of God's protection, away from the centre of His will. That was why Satan had been able to put the awful illness upon me only days later. Again I heard the voice of God saying, 'YOU MUST GIVE THE MESSAGE TO THE CHURCH' just before He miraculously healed me. Now I knew and understood. I had to warn the people of the world of the days in which we were living and urge His children to be wise in these end-times. I had to preach His message, regardless of whether it was received with gladness. As never before, I saw that my calling was to OBEY GOD, and not to please man. I can now praise the Lord for the typhoid fever for if I had not endured such a harsh chastening for my disobedience, I know that I should have turned my back on this message through fear of man and the natural, human desire to be loved and accepted.

That evening, I was asked to share my testimony about what the Lord was doing in the Philippines and the work of the Mission. When the offering was brought round, I put in my last fourteen dollars. But God is no man's debtor. At the end of the evening, six hundred dollars had been given to send back to the Philippines for the hungry orphans and the Bible students.

The following morning the telephone rang and I was surprised when I heard the call, 'Isabel, it's for you.' I was even more surprised when I heard a husky male voice on the other end of the line saying, 'You won't know me, but I was in church last night and heard you preach. I'm very impressed with your ministry and I really feel it's the Lord's will that we meet and get to know each other. Will you come and have dinner with me tomorrow evening?'

He must have heard me gasp and gulp rather confusedly, for he added quickly, 'Do Bring Pastor and Mrs Browning along too.'

So it was all arranged and, feeling rather like Cinderella, I duly travelled with the pastor and his wife to the grandest hotel in Des Moines. It seemed a foregone conclusion that our mystery host should be a tall, dark businessman in a well-cut suit who exuded an air of confidence and ease. The meal was a banquet and my head felt as if it was on a swivel as I stared round at the exotic food, the lavish interior and, most of all, the waiters wearing bow-ties and tails. The conversation was quite general, mostly about our host's life and the work of the Lord in the area, and in fact I said very little, happy just to absorb our breathtaking surroundings.

A few days later I was overwhelmed when the dear brother arrived laden with gifts to help me in my ministry: cameras, travelling bags, books and cassettes. Before I could recover, he asked me to have lunch with him the following day, and I nodded mutely.

Next day, as I was dressing for my luncheon date, a thought was suddenly firmly planted in my mind: 'He is going to ask you to marry him!' Thunderstruck, I just fell on my knees and cried out to the Lord, 'Father, is this *your* will for me?' Straight into my mind came the words, 'My grace is sufficient for thee.' But before I could ask Him what He meant by that, the brother was ringing the door bell.

I got in his car and we drove to the same grand hotel. No sooner had we started lunch than he pushed his plate aside and said in a rush, 'Isabel, the Lord has told me that you are to be my wife!'

I am glad the Lord had prepared me or I would have choked on my soup. Before I could reply, he plunged on with great eagerness, explaining in detail the sort of ministry we would share and the happiness we would have. I sat there, hardly daring to open my mouth in case I said the wrong thing. As he rushed on excitedly, I just prayed silently in tongues all the time, reaching out to the Lord to know His will. Gradually fear and unrest began to creep into my heart and I recalled that the Lord had told me to live one day at a time and not to plan for the future as only He knew what the future would hold. I gazed at this earnest young man. He had a good and kind heart and at that point I knew that he really believed that I was to be his wife. I shrank at the thought of hurting his feelings, but as the uneasiness within me grew stronger, I knew without doubt that it was not the Lord's will for me to marry this man.

At last I gathered enough courage to speak, and without any preamble I said simply, 'When the Lord tells me that I am to be your wife, then we'll do something about it. Until that happens, it would be better if we don't meet.'

He seemed quite happy with that statement, seeming to take it for granted that I would soon be given the same message, and he drove me back to the pastor's house in good spirits, still full of enthusiasm for our life together. It wasn't to be. Soon afterwards the Lord let me out of that state I never saw him again.

The following Wednesday was the big night at Kingsway Cathedral, a church which struck me by its glorious freedom from denominational ties and prejudices. Academic awards for theological students connected with the church were to be presented, and I was adorned in doctorate robes to receive Revd Shields's degree. It was my duty to stand and address the congregation on his behalf and I did so, conscious of the great privilege of speaking in the place of such a mighty man of God. For thirty-four years, he had fulfilled his calling as missionary to the Philippines, ministering and teaching God's Word, establishing and supervising Miracle Mission until it became known all over the world. Then the ministers of the church laid hands on me, praying God's anointing upon my own ministry. Such a weighty commission could not be received lightly, and under the power of the Holy Spirit the feeling left my legs as the ministers prayed, and I sank to the floor, beholding nothing except His glory.

My brief stay in Des Moines was a blessed time, for God my Father seemed intent on giving me what I had not expected, material comforts and pleasures that I had long forgotten: 'I will give you what you have not asked for' (I Kings 3: 13). From hiking up mountain tracks, wading through leech-infested paddy fields, struggling through jungle undergrowth, sleeping on hard bamboo floors and bathing in muddy pools, I was transported to the luxury of beautifully furnished homes, private swimming pools, and being driven around in Cadillacs. But the recent months had taught me to be able to say with Paul: 'I have learned the secret of being content in any and every situation, whether well-fed or hungry, whether living in plenty or in want' (Phil. 4: 12). I was grateful to the Lord for these unlooked-for gifts, but in my heart I knew that they were nothing compared with the 'surpassing greatness of knowing Christ Jesus my Lord' (Phil. 3: 8).

My time was in God's hands, and He led me next to a fellowship in Brighton, Michigan, pastored by Revd and Mrs Doorn. Hours after arriving in their home, I felt a great burden weighing down upon my heart, and although I did not understand its cause, I spent much of the night on my knees, crying out to the Lord in tongues, allowing the Holy Spirit to intercede for me in this unknown problem. The heaviness did not depart the following morning, and all I could do was remain on my knees. After hours of prayer, the burden lifted, and in that moment, the Spirit revealed to me that I should go on a fast connected in some way with Mrs Doorn, the pastor's wife. When I told her that the Lord was telling me to go on a fast for her, she admitted that she had osteoarthritis and was in considerable pain for most of the time. A strong conviction filled me that God would heal her, but that in this chronic case His purposes were to be implemented through prayer and fasting. For one, two, three, four, five days I touched no food and drank only the minimum of liquid until on the afternoon of the fifth day I felt a sudden release and a clear assurance that there was no need to fast any longer.

I found Mrs Doorn in the garden picking strawberries

with evident pain and difficulty, and it was obvious that she neither looked nor felt any better. Still, I had learnt that we walk by faith, led by the Spirit, not by sight or reason, and God's Word was all the ground we needed to be able to stand in confidence that His healing power was at work according to His own inscrutable wisdom. We went into the house and Mrs Doorn prepared a bowl of clear soup for me to minimise the shock of food to my body after days of abstinence. As I sipped it slowly with deep enjoyment, Pastor Doorn arrived home with the news that a well-known preacher would be speaking at a meeting that night and suggested that we all went to hear him.

No sooner had we entered the hall than I felt a stirring excitement in my heart and I knew that something tremendous was going to happen that night. A powerful time of praise and worship gave way to the ministry of the preacher and, even as he stood, the mantle of God fell upon him. Walking down the aisle, he pointed to someone in the congregation who rose, rather hesitantly, 'You have been suffering from a heart condition,' said the preacher, simply and calmly, not asking a question but merely delivering a piece of inspired knowledge.

'Yes, that's true,' replied the man in wonder. The preacher stretched out his hand and laid it on the man's head saying in a voice of authority, 'Be healed in the name of Jesus!' Down went the restored man under the touch of God, and a few minutes later he got up and raised his hands joyfully in the air, thanking Jesus for delivering him from the heart disease.

I was not surprised when, a moment later, the preacher suddenly looked in our direction and called Mrs Doorn out to the front. But I was unprepared for the next dramatic event, for suddenly, with my physical eyes, I saw an evil spirit before me, a grotesque black shape which hissed malevolently, 'Now we shall see how you like it.' Instantly I felt an excruciating pain in my right shoulder so that I gasped in agony. Reaching out for the strength of the Lord, I began to take authority over that evil thing.

'I bind you in the name of Jesus, and command that you

depart from me by the power in the blood of Jesus shed on Calvary.' The demon vanished, and I became aware of the preacher standing by my side. To my astonishment, he took me by the hand and raised me to my feet. Then laying his hand on my forehead, he said, 'That for which you have been fasting has been fulfilled!' For the next few minutes my spirit was caught up with joy and praise to God. My thanksgiving was soon doubled when I found Mrs Doorn glorifying the Lord beside me for the complete deliverance from all pain and illness she had been experiencing.

# Chapter Twenty-Two

It was July 1981, ten months after that memorable Full Gospel Businessmen's dinner when I gave my life to the Lord. I spent most of the hot weeks travelling from state to state with the Doorn family as the pastor journeyed around preaching, teaching and ministering. The Lord opened many doors for me to speak and give my testimony, demonstrating His commitment to His Word by the signs and wonders that followed. I had sought simply to be obedient to the prompting of His Spirit, ministering and preaching as He led, looking to Him only for the needs of the moment. But at one service in a large church, which was powerfully moving on in the Spirit, the Lord gave me an unlooked-for blessing and encouragement by a public declaration of His covering over my life. The pastor's son, who had never met me, suddenly walked over to me and began to prophesy before the whole congregation, bringing Word from the Lord which greatly enlarged my vision of the way ahead. The entire service was taped, and I offer the prophecy here word for word as it has been transcribed so that you may weigh in your own spirit this revelation of the Lord's purposes:

'... I have called you, my daughter. You have heard the cry, but you have not seen and you have not heard what I will lead you into; you have just heard the cry. Part of thy work, my daughter, is this: you are going to be a repairer of the breach, though at the moment you do not understand what the breach is. The breach is in the kingdom of God.

I have picked you because you have heard me say that I shall show my glory in the earth, regardless of men and religiosity. You shall stand and you shall be open, and I shall reveal my purposes to you. You will not only know me as Christ, but you will know me as a deliverer, and as a Father of Israel before all is

125

done. You will be to me as a son, and not only as a bride. You will know me as the God of the universe, for I have shown you but an inkling, yes, only a jot and a tittle of what my wonders can perform.

I have picked you and lifted you up because of your obedience and because of your heart. I have set you in a realm of victory. My Word shall find a stable place in your heart wherever you go. You may feel as Jeremiah when he said, 'Lord, I am only a youth; they will not listen to me.' But I tell you that Israel had hardened her heart at that time and would not listen to the truth of her deliverance. As for you, I shall take you and I shall confound the men who set themselves as the scribes and Pharisees and Saducees of this day. I shall show the revelation of Jesus Christ in you, and you shall be used in this day. For there are those whose hearts have been hardened by the education they have received, because of the ways of the world that have been taught them, and they have closed their hearts to the truth.

But I shall take delight in you, my daughter, because of the simplicity of my Word in your heart, because of the truth that is within you. You will perform my works, and you will see the Lord of Hosts revealed, not only in you yourself, but in your dwelling-place, in your circumstances, and wherever you go. My glory will be revealed in an ever greater realm, and as you see these things, you will understand that you are truly a son. For I will bring you into a blessing and a dimension that you have not yet known because I have declared that my kingdom will be established for ever and ever, and even if a man came as an angel he could never take it away.

For you shall be used. Harken to my Word, and it shall not only set you free, but it shall set men free too. Yes, my daughter, the fire of the Lord shall surround you, and you shall do greater works than all which have gone before. Have you not heard that greater than these which I have done, you will do because I have gone to the Father? You will stand amazed at what God will perform through you, for do you not know that you are appointed by me, that you are a special vessel unto me? Fear not, my daughter, for though people rise up against you, every tongue that speaks against you will be condemned by you, for this is the prerogative of the saints. I have called you in due time, for these are the end-days and you will be faithful. Greater things shall come forth than you have performed before, through your word, through your lips. You shall see mighty miracles and multitudes will come unto God because you have been faithful to my Word,

126

for it shall not return unto me void. I have given this into your care, and you shall go forth mightily to do and to conquer because you go in my name, says the Lord your God who loves you.'

At Illinois, we attended a Christian convention where a woman from the congregation testified to God's grace in saving her life. She was a medical doctor, and on returning unexpectedly to the surgery two nights before, she had surprised a group of thieves who had presumably broken in to steal drugs. She managed to raise the alarm just as they seized her and held a knife to her throat, threatening to kill her. Help arrived in the nick of time, but not before her arm had been so badly twisted behind her that it had been broken in three places.

While she was speaking, I found myself walking over to her as she drew her testimony to a close. I laid my hand on the injured arm and prayed, 'Father, in the name of Jesus, I ask you to knit these bones together.' Instantly the arm was healed, and in a few moments the sling and plaster were off, and the woman was joyfully waving her arm in all directions.

God's work in connection with this woman expanded beyond the miracle of her restored arm. It was becoming daily more apparent that God was consolidating a message in my heart through the experiences and the people I met. I told Dr Johnson that I was going to leave Illinois and travel to another convention at St Louis with Pastor and Mrs Doorn. On the spur of the moment, she decided that she would attend the conference too, so to keep her company we arranged that I should travel in her car, following the Doorns to our destination.

God does not waste time. As we travelled, this young doctor could talk of nothing but the second coming of Jesus, and the Scriptures pertaining to the rise of the Antichrist and the mark of the Beast. It was sobering to learn that the medical authorities in the States had been lecturing their staff on the usage of a type of laser pen which was to be implemented shortly by doctors to mark the patient's body prior to treatment. Whatever was written was invisible to the human eye and could be seen only when a certain sort of light was shone over the area. How easily this laser method of tattoo could be used commercially or politically to mark people with a registration, identity or account number!

Dr Johnson also told me that only three weeks before she had done something she had never done in her life – stopped to pick up a complete stranger on the highway. As they got into conversation she realised that he was a Christian, and all he spoke about was the certainty that Jesus was coming back soon. At a petrol station, she stopped the car and got out to ask the attendant to fill up the tank, but when she turned back to speak to her passenger, she found to her amazement that he had just disappeared.

'Did you see where my companion went?' she asked the attendant, who looked at her most oddly and replied, 'Lady, you were the only one in the car when you drove in here!' The doctor was flabbergasted. She knew she had picked up the stranger and that he had told her with assurance that we were living in the last days. Braving the curious stare of the attendant, she asked him to look in the men's lavatory, but the place was empty. With quiet conviction, Dr Johnson looked me straight in the eye and said, 'I am sure the stranger was an angel sent by God to tell us to prepare ourselves for the coming of the Lord Jesus. No one knows the day nor the hour, but we can be certain it's very near!'

We had been travelling for hours along the straight, dusty highways of the United States, always keeping the Doorns' bronze-coloured car just in front. But at some point our excitement must have broken our concentration, for suddenly we realised that the Doorns' car was nowhere in sight. Thinking that our speed must have dropped as we talked, the doctor pressed her foot down on the accelerator and we shot forward. After thirty minutes' speeding down the interminable highway, we had to face the awful fact that we were lost. At that speed we should surely have caught them up by now, and we had to conclude that they must have turned off without our noticing.

'Never mind,' said Dr Johnson cheerfully, 'I'm sure we can find our own way to the convention.'

'It won't be that easy,' I replied ruefully, 'I'm afraid I never found out where it was to be held!'

Our hearts sank as we pictured the huge city of St Louis. We didn't even know the name of the convention. There was only one thing to do. Bringing the car to a standstill at the roadside, we simply poured out our hearts to the Lord. 'Father,' I prayed, 'we're completely lost. Please *somehow* get us back behind the Doorns' car.'

I had hesitated about including in the book what happened next as I was sure that people would disbelieve it, but God has shown me that I must give Him the glory due to His name. We both began to pray in tongues and soon became immersed in the Spirit, unconscious of everything except that we were in heavenly places with the Lord. At the same instant, we stopped praying and opened our eyes. To our amazement we were driving along the highway and there, directly in front of us, was the Doorns' car! Dr Johnson had certainly never switched on the car and moved out on to the road, and neither of us had been aware of any movement. We can give no explanation except that the mighty hand of our heavenly Father had intervened and translated us in a moment of time back behind our travelling companions.

We sang praises to the Lord all the way to St Louis, arriving at our destination stiff and tired after such a long journey, but with our spirits soaring.

'What happened to you?' asked Pastor Doorn when we got out of the car. 'I kept looking in the mirror for you but you were nowhere to be seen. Then, out of the blue, you just appeared!' Joyfully we told him our story, and he, too, believed that it was God who had caught us up into the air and set us down behind his car. When our tour was ended and we were back in Brighton, Michigan, Pastor Doorn shared the wonder of our translation to his whole church and Dr Johnson testified to it.

In St Louis we also attended a women's convention and exactly the same message was preached – the Antichrist, the mark of the Beast and the return of Jesus. With 'coincidences' too numerous to credit, I had not a shadow of doubt that the reason the Lord had brought me to the United States was to confirm and instruct me further in the message He wanted me to give His people.

# Chapter Twenty-Three

I returned with Pastor and Mrs Doorn to their home, and at once received a telephone call from the Philippines. Revd Shields needed help. A typhoon had hit the islands and towns had been plunged into darkness as hurricane winds tore down communications and power lines. Highways were strewn with fallen trees and tidal waves had wiped out an entire town leaving twenty-nine dead and thousands homeless. The Lord had protected Miracle Mission from any damage and no one had been hurt, but they were inundated with stricken people and orphaned children. As we listened to the news, God touched Mrs Doorn's heart and she knew she had to go there to help. After a time of prayer, the Lord's plan for our return was confirmed and we made immediate preparations for the journey.

By the time we arrived in Sanfernando, the worst of the confusion caused by the typhoon had subsided, but there was great distress and more than eighty students and orphans had been added to the numbers at the Mission. None of these children knew the Lord Jesus as their Saviour, so a special service was arranged for the newcomers. No wonder the Lord loves these little ones. In their openness and simplicity, they welcomed the message of a Father in heaven who loved them and would care for them always. From three years upwards, the children earnestly asked Jesus to come into their hearts. Mrs Doorn and I laid hands on these reborn babes, and asked Jesus to fill them with His Holy Spirit. It was a memory I shall always treasure, for as the Spirit moved among them they fell to the ground, lost in the joy of being able to talk with their father in His own heavenly language. A unique atmosphere of purity and grace reigned as Jesus became real to these children and they loved and worshipped their Saviour.

I remembered the words in the book of Joel, 'In the last days I will pour out my spirit on *all* flesh.' In the coming days, the children learnt that they could sing praises to God in their new tongues – and there was no stopping them! For long periods of time, these young ones would be abandoned in worship of their Father who had lifted them from despair into the security of His kingdom. Often I saw tears of joy running down their faces as they prayed.

The day finally came when the money to buy the new jeep had been changed from English pounds into American dollars and then into Philippine pesos, that way ensuring the best rate of exchange. Having unreservedly surrendered my last penny to the Lord for His work here, I was overwhelmed when Pastor Doorn's church insisted on paying me back half the cost of the jeep. Amid shouts of excitement, the new Toyota jeep arrived, gleaming, at the Mission. As we laid hands on it to dedicate it to the Lord for His service in bringing souls into His kingdom, someone touched my shoulder and began to prophesy. The message of promised blessing and provision moved me so deeply that it was difficult to recall afterwards the specific words, except that the Lord vowed there would always be money in a bank account for me, and that sometimes I would never know where it came from. Right up until this moment I have never known financial want, for God has always ensured that there has been enough money for my immediate need, and I know His supply will never fail until the day comes when we shall no longer be able to buy or sell.

Soon the Lord called back the sister He had given me for these precious weeks, and I accompanied Mrs Doorn to the airport to get her flight home to her husband and family. After a loving farewell, I boarded a jeepney to take me to the bus station to catch the bus to Laguna, the next town to which the Spirit of God was calling me.

My travelling companions on this jeep were dressed in green and white uniforms and, when I saw they were carrying Bibles, I realised they must be students of a Bible college. I began to share with them the message about the

Lord's return, and as I spoke I could feel the anointing of the Lord come down. Two of the girls began to cry quietly, and although I did not understand why they were crying I put my arms round their shoulders to comfort them. As I prayed in tongues, Jesus touched the girls with the baptism of His Holy Spirit, and they just slithered off the seats on to their knees in the back of the jeep, singing praises to God in a language which sounded beautiful and heavenly.

As the jeep continued to trundle through the busy streets of Manila, I laid hands on all the students, and the Lord did a wonderful work in their hearts, giving them all a new language to praise Him with. Suddenly I realised that the jeep had stopped and the bemused face of the driver appeared round the door, wanting to know what all the commotion was about. Since he could speak English, I invited him to join us in the back.

He didn't stand much chance in that atmosphere. Within five minutes he, too, had been filled with the Spirit! For two hours we had wonderful fellowship in the back of the jeep on a busy main road in the centre of Manila. The traffic was roaring past and people stared in at us with curiosity, but it did not matter; we were in the presence of Almighty God. These students were praising the Lord in a way they never knew possible, and had been set free to put their arms round each other and share a new dimension of love. God revealed to me that He was healing resentment and bitterness which had grown in their hearts towards one another, but now all that was healed and they were even prophesying to each other! When the anointing lifted, they were full of questions, for they had never seen or heard before that the Holy Spirit could work in such a way. I took them to the Scriptures, and let His Word answer all their questions.

From there I boarded a rickety old bus which was to take me to Laguna. Laguna was a particularly vice-ridden town, and it was a surprise to find that the only missionaries there were two remarkable women, Sister Mahaan and Sister Susan. But I found them low and discouraged. They were fighting a fierce spiritual battle against witchcraft and idol worship and the going was tough. I soon realised that the

Lord had sent me there to give them some encouragement and build them up.

They had no church building so they met in people's homes. The first evening we gathered in someone's house and from the start we had a tremendous assurance that God was going to work mightily in that area. Even in that meeting, we saw a wonderful demonstration of the moving of the Holy Spirit in people's lives.

The following day we travelled by foot to a place called San Francisco, no more than a primitive village, despite its grand name. There the inhabitants made their living from the coconut trees. It was fascinating to watch the men cutting down the coconuts with sharp knives attached to long bamboo poles, but it was also very dangerous as one had to keep well out of the way when the bunches of coconuts came crashing to the ground with a mighty thud. The nuts were then gathered up and carried to a large hut where the husks were stripped off, some to be used in weaving mats, and some smouldered over a fire to make charcoal.

A favourite use of the coconut tree was for brewing coconut wine, and this they would risk their lives for, shinning up huge trunks to cut incisions in the tree at the top. There they would insert a bamboo drain pipe to extract the liquid which would have formed the coconut. With this liquid, they made a very potent wine, but sadly, when a tree has been doctored in this way it never again bears coconuts.

The two missionary sisters had a great burden for the people of this village for they were bound by forces of evil which kept them in a tight grip of idol worship. They had a church but it was adorned with idols of their patron saint, St Francis. The people prayed to the statues and believed that when the idol was in deep intercession, it actually perspired on its forehead. The Holy Spirit could not move there for they were not prepared to give up their idols, so all we could do was minister to the children, telling them Jesus loved them, and teaching them gospel choruses.

It was so refreshing to visit the next remote village of Taytay. The anointing of the Lord was tremendous for the people were open to receive Him and the Holy Spirit was able to move in a dramatic way. The church was so tiny that the villagers could not all get in, but the doors were flung wide and they all heard the gospel, and fifty souls repented of their sins. As the Holy Spirit began to minister to the people, they fell to the ground inside the church and even outside on the pathways, and we saw many miracles as God met individual needs. One woman had a growth in her breast which instantly disappeared in the name of Jesus Christ; a pregnant woman was in terrible pain and they feared she was having a miscarriage, but she was released from it as soon as I laid my hands on her stomach and asked the Lord to bring a healthy baby from the mother's womb; a man had been paralysed with a stroke down one side, and after prayer was able to move his arm freely for the first time in years. There were many other healings as God proved His faithfulness to His Word.

Back in Laguna, I was taken to visit another family who wanted to hear about Jesus. As I sat and shared with them that Jesus's love had led Him to die for them on the Cross, the door opened and in walked an attractive young girl in her teens. Her face was as white as a sheet and I noticed that she had a large piece of plaster stuck on her neck. When I asked her why the plaster was there, she explained that she had just come from seeing a faith healer, for she had discovered a goitre growing in her neck, disfiguring her young beauty. The faith healer had persuaded her that if she paid him some money, he would be able to rid her of the goitre for ever. She had been made to lie down on a couch, and the man knelt and prayed to the many idols which adorned the room. Then he took a razor blade dipped in hot water and made a cut in her neck about two inches long. Putting his mouth to the opening, he sucked the lumps out of her flesh and spat them into a jar. She held out a jar of murky liquid, and floating in the middle were two dark bloody blobs.

I felt intensely sick as I heard this gruesome tale and I began to pray quietly in tongues. Then I laid my hands on her and asked the Lord to heal all that had been damaged. Instantly she fell to the ground under the power of Almighty God. For twenty minutes she lay there motionless looking deathly white. Then the colour began to creep back into her face, and when she opened her eyes she was glowing. Jesus had healed her! Gently I led her in a prayer of repentance and she accepted Jesus as her Lord and Saviour.

After experiences like these, it was not difficult to understand why my two dear sisters were feeling discouraged. I had never encountered an area where witchcraft and spiritism had such dominion. Having called these two women, God had equipped them for the spiritual battle and souls were being saved, but the fight was taking a toll on their courage and strength. I wished that others could be found to stand with them in this struggle, for Satan seemed to be adding to his numbers every day as well. While I was there we heard of a new radio programme run by a man called Johnny Midnight. He openly declared that he was a witch and that he had gone to the great city of London to learn all there was to know about the magic arts. During one broadcast, he announced that if there was anyone in need of healing, they must put a glass of water on top of the radio. Then, when he made a strange sound, they were to drink the water and would find that they were healed.

To our astonishment, we began to meet people who had listened to this programme and were testifying to the fact that they had been healed. How could we convince these people that this man was evil when they had been released from their sickness and pain by listening to his programme? We sought the Lord in prayer and then went back to the people with His answer. As it was the Devil who had put the disease upon them in the first place, it was easy for him to take it away. We explained that the Devil's only objective is to kill, steal and destroy; even if he took their illness away for the meantime, something much worse would come upon them in the future. I read to them from God's Word: 'The Spirit clearly says that in later times some will abandon the faith and follow deceiving spirits and things taught by demons' (1 Timothy 4: 1).

I explained that we were living in the last days and the Devil was trying to get as many people as he could to follow him so that they should spend eternity with him in the lake of fire. Salvation, wholeness and everlasting life was what Jesus offered, and many of the people became convinced that He was the only way, and repented of their sins, being born again of God's Spirit. Before I left the area, I knelt with these new brothers and sisters, and together we asked the Lord to send His Holy Spirit to convict Johnny Midnight of his sins and show him the error of his ways.

By the time I returned to Miracle Mission, I had seen hundreds of souls bow the knee to the one, true, living God. In obedience to the command of Jesus that those who believe should be baptised, we always found the nearest river and baptised the new converts there in the name of the Father, Son and Holy Spirit so that they would be able to stand in the coming days as new creations raised to walk in newness of life with Christ Jesus, their old natures buried for ever in His death.

My visa was due to expire and it was time to ask the Lord whether He wanted me to return to Britain or continue to serve Him out in the Philippines. I thought of Britain with warmth, but my home was in God's kingdom and I prayed, 'You know my heart, Lord. I only want to be where you want me to be. If it is your will that I go back to England at this time, then please supply my fare.' I was at peace, for I knew that He would show me the right course and in His plan lay my highest good and blessing.

During the days of waiting I stayed in Manila, the capital, with a lovely Filipino family whose lives had been transformed by the Spirit of the Lord. On most days, we visited from house to house, healing the sick and sharing the good news of God's eternal life.

On one occasion I was taken to pray for a woman dying of an incurable tropical disease. The first thing that met me as I walked through the door, was an altar bedecked with idols and statues, new and costly, in sharp contrast to the dirt and poverty of the hovel which housed them. On a wooden bed in a corner lay the sick woman, a few filthy rags covering her wasted body. She tossed feverishly in the thick heat and small moans rasped through her cracked lips. The seat which was offered to me by a member of her family was a bizarre creation, pieces of wood of all shapes and sizes, thrown together with a few crude nails. A large picture of the Virgin Mary hung incongruously on the wall above the bed. As I moved to the woman's side, a large rat disappeared under the bed, and I quietly sat with my feet pointing away from the creature's hiding place. I noticed a bag of market vegetables and provisions into which mice were climbing freely and rummaging noisily among the shopping. The air was hot and humid, heavy with foul smells, and my mind clouded under the onslaught of all these sensations. But as I looked to the Lord, He lifted me above my surroundings and gave me the message that was to be life for that woman. It was a laboured process, for every word had to be interpreted, but I explained the error of idol worship to the woman and the whole family who had gathered for her approaching death, and described the holiness of God who created the heaven and the earth and gave life to all people through His Son.

Every minute was precious for the sick woman's strength was ebbing fast, but now, as the message of God's love and goodness stole into her mind and spirit, her body too was touched by His restoring power. The entire family were soon kneeling to repent of their sins and commit their lives to God, and the sick woman looked and felt a new person in body and soul. Solemnly they promised that the idols would be destroyed and they would henceforth worship only the one, true Lord who had risen from the dead.

Closer and closer drew the expiry date of my visa but still no clear leading from the Lord. Just before the deadline, I was taken to a convention of Spirit-filled ministers from all over the island. The chairman invited me to address the meeting, and never had I felt such a strong leading to share the message about the return of Jesus and the rise of the Antichrist. At the end of it, a great sense of peace and fulfilment rested on me, and I realised that through this convention, God had given His message to men who would faithfully carry it to the Church in every corner of the country. My work here was completed for the present time, and I almost expected the letters which arrived the following day, one from England and one from America. It was like coming to the last page of a book one has read before. The church in Norwich had taken up an offering and sent £250 for me and £100 towards food for the orphans. The envelope from the United States contained $160. My heart expanded in praise. The money came to the exact amount for my fare to Britain. I was going home.

## Chapter Twenty-Four

My future lay in the mind of God but He had provided for the present through the invitation of a dear Christian friend to stay with her as I waited on the Lord for His direction. This presented an interesting test of where the foundation of my life really lay, for Maria lived across the road from where I used to live before I sold my home and went out to the Philippines. I wondered what I should feel when I saw my home inhabited by someone else, and as the taxi drove slowly past the bungalow it seemed as if time had stood still. Nothing had changed, the garden looked just the same, and I could almost imagine walking up the path and unlocking the front door as if the past few months had been only a dream. Then I saw a figure in the sitting room draw the curtains on the outside world, blotting out my past, and the realisation that the bungalow no longer belonged to me came forcibly home. Yet I had no regrets, not a single one. The desire of my heart was not to own houses or land, but to serve God, and if that meant living out of a suitcase, then out of a suitcase I should live, knowing that in God's plan I should have complete fulfilment.

As we drove on past, a Scripture was strongly impressed on my mind: 'In my Father's house are many mansions . . . I go to prepare a place for you.' More and more I was seeing that I was just passing through this world, and as I set my eyes and heart firmly on things above, so I was experiencing a deeper sense of peace and freedom than I had ever known. If it was God's will that I move from place to place, then I knew He would supply all my needs. If He desired that I should have a home, then that would bring me equal happiness. With joy I realised afresh that my treasure was in heaven and not in the world. I had the confidence of David in God's provision:

'Lord, you have assigned me my portion and
my cup, you have made my lot secure.
The boundary lines have fallen for me in
pleasant places;
surely I have a delightful inheritance.' (Ps. 16: 5-6).


I was longing to share with everyone the mighty miracles
God had performed out in the Philippines, and to lead others
into the experience of His power to heal, deliver and save,
but I soon met with a phenomenon I was not expecting.

People listened and said politely, 'How wonderful', yet
their enthusiasm was often tempered by the statement that,
of course, God does not work like that in this country. I was
astounded. The God who had worked such miracles in the
Philippines was the same God people worshipped in
England. The apostles in the book of Acts performed signs
and wonders in the same name. Neither God nor His love
changed according to the time or place. Yet when I was
sharing my testimony, I often felt a barrier of doubt and
unbelief. There was so little openness to the possibility of
healing and miraculous provision that after a while I began
to wonder if they weren't right in a way – God was *unable* to
work the same miracles in England.

I received a similar negative response to the message
concerning the urgency for Christians to prepare for the
return of the Lord Jesus and to be aware of the evil forces so
subtly at work in these last days. I was rocking the boat.
Many people refused to leave their undramatic but
comfortable Christian life-styles to step into something so
challenging. Others were fearful of a message so radical and
uncompromising, whether it concerned the imminent
dissolution of this world order, or the power of God that can
be loosed in a life totally surrendered to Him. For whatever
reasons, the people among whom I first learnt of the Lord
now rejected the message I had returned from the
Philippines to share, although their goodwill towards me
remained.

The Holy Spirit's call throughout the Scriptures is for ears
that will hear. God does not force Himself upon hearts which

are hardened to His voice. In a remarkable way, He began to open another door for me when the one in my home area remained steadfastly closed. Out of the blue I received a cheque for £50 from a couple living in Devon, whom I had met at a wedding in Norwich, Geoffrey and Tina Campbell-Black. I knew the money was for something specific, and I was sure that God would soon show me His plan.

A few days later I visited a couple who had been clients of mine when I was employed by the insurance company. I shared my testimony with them and, to my joy, God's words answered a thirst in their lives and they repented of their sins, receiving Jesus as their Saviour. Before I left their home that evening, they showed me a new electric organ of which they were very proud. Their only problem was that they had not been able to sell their old one, even though it was in perfect working order. To my surprise, the Lord spoke to me and told me to buy the organ. But to check that I was hearing Him aright, I asked the man how much he was asking for it. 'Fifty pounds,' came the reply and I knew at once that God was not joking, even though I could not play the organ and did not even have a home to put it in! I could only assume He wanted me to learn the instrument and I marvelled at the originality of His ideas.

The following day I was invited to a house group in Great Yarmouth where people had expressed a great interest in what God had been doing in the Philippines. For the first time since I returned, I saw the power of God moving mightily in people's lives. Whether the need was physical healing or spiritual anointing, the Lord's touch met each one, and many fell to the ground as His Spirit overwhelmed them and Jesus became real in their lives.

At the meeting I was asked if I would go and pray for the father of one of the women in the house group. The following afternoon I went and ministered to him and had the joy of leading him into a deeper walk with his Lord. As we sat drinking tea together after we had prayed, the old gentleman began to reminisce about his youth and the pleasure he used to find in tinkling on the keys of an organ. 'For the past couple of months I've had such a desire to take it up again. But there's no chance of it,' he sighed. 'I'm too old now, I expect, and besides, these organs cost a fair bit of money nowadays.'

My heart leapt, but I did not say anything to the old man until I had arranged with his daughter to collect the organ and take it round to her father the next day. When he discovered that the dream of his old age had become a reality, he could hardly contain his emotion. And when I explained with all honesty that it was the Lord's plan, not mine, sheer joy and wonder spread across his face as it registered that his Saviour Jesus had given him the desire of his heart.

Strangely, it was this organ which opened the door to the ministry that has occupied me up to this date. I should never have been prompted to go to the south-west of England by my own thought and reasoning as I knew nothing about the area. But God knew that His Word and purposes would find a receptivity there. I telephoned Geoffrey and Tina Campbell-Black to describe to them the joy of their gift and their own obedience to God had brought in the life of one lonely old man. Their vicar and his wife happened to be visiting at the time, and I was invited to come to their church and give my testimony. The Lord gave them far more than my testimony. The openness of the people in that area enabled Him to move in a remarkable way, restoring broken bodies, spirits and relationships with His healing touch.

Since then God has taken me to many parts of England and I have seen the power of Jesus at work as lives have been transformed and filled with the Holy Spirit. People healed and delivered in the mighty name of Jesus. Thousands have been born again of the Spirit of God as His prophetic Word has broken down barriers of fear and unbelief. Sadly, sometimes voices have risen in opposition and unbelief. God promised that too. Nevertheless, His kingdom has been extended, and fellowship given fresh vision and encouragement as they have come into a fuller understanding of His purposes in these days. Wherever I go, God has confirmed to me the truth of the message concerning the imminent return of the Lord Jesus, for I find

He has laid the same burden on the hearts of many other men and women who are seeking to know His mind and understand the signs of the times. Christians are searching the Scriptures and reaching out to the Spirit for His interpretation of the prophecies related to these things, no longer depending on learned theologians to interpret these truths. The Lord is not a cruel God who will allow the horror of the end-times to fall on His children unawares. He has made provision for His people to be prepared – and the answer lies in His Word.

There is nothing new or contrived about this message. It has been written in the Scriptures for centuries, and Christians all over the world are realising that what they thought were myths and pictures have a literalness and relevance that is crucial to their spiritual survival. Satan has developed many ways of distracting the attention of God's people from His kingdom, and there has been none so subtle as deceiving the members of the Body of Christ into a false security that they will be taken out of the world before any persecution. Persecution is already here. Half the Body of Christ is living in countries where there is no liberty to worship God. Thousands of Christians are imprisoned today in labour camps and institutions, being beaten and tortured daily. There is a law in Russia which forbids parents to give their children a Christian education. If they do, the authorities take the children away and place them in atheistic schools. The Body of Christ is already enduring terrible suffering. In the Western world, fear has gripped the hearts of many believers who know that persecution is coming to them. The Holy Spirit is seeking to do a work of preparation which will overcome fear, but our hearts and minds must be open to accept the truth – that persecution is coming to all who belong to Jesus.

I am convinced that this world's time has almost run out. This is the generation which will see the destruction of this present world order, and the establishment of the Lord's kingdom. It is a glorious time to be living! But it is also a time when many will be deceived and many unprepared so that thousands will miss their salvation or faint from fear in the days of tribulation. This is why I offer in the last part of this book a summary of the message God has told me to give to the Church. It is the fruit of countless hours spent studying His Word and seeking His understanding. Some elements you may feel are my own conjecture, but the essence of the message comes directly from the Spirit of God, and I humbly direct you to the Scriptures to find for yourselves the description of our present world situation and the pattern of the events soon to come. No theological training or intellectual brilliance is required; only an openness and a dedication of time, concentration and prayer. Then I believe you will share the same urgency to warn those who still live in darkness that the kingdom of God is at hand, and to encourage His people to step into the authority that is theirs and exercise the power that is available through the name of Jesus. *Maranatha!*

*Epilogue*

# End-Time Message

*We are living in the last days of the world as we know it. The times of the Gentiles are on the very brink of fulfilment. The Lord God of Israel will lead every Jew from all the countries where He has scattered them, including hundreds of thousands from Russia, home to their Promised Land. The greatest prophecies of all time are being fulfilled before your eyes. In the clouds of heaven, in great glory and power, Christ will return for His Bride. THE LORD JESUS IS COMING BACK SOON!*

*The earth's resources are rapidly running out; the trend of men's hearts is turned towards evil. In spite of an increase in knowledge, human nature has become a slave to violence, hatred, rebellion, immoral practices, fornication, adultery and homosexuality, all of which are a disgust to God, but have become the modern way in which we live. Society no longer rejects such behaviour, and many churches no longer preach against it, but rather encourage people in their perverted sexual activities, as it was in the days of Noah, when the Lord God saw the extent of human wickedness and that the trend and direction of men's lives were only towards evil. He was sorry that He had made man. It broke His heart, and He said,*

'I will blot out from the face of the earth all mankind that I have created.'

*Now Noah was a pleasure to the Lord; he was the only truly righteous man living on earth at that time. As God observed that all mankind was vicious and depraved, He said to Noah,*

'I have decided to destroy all mankind, for the earth is filled with crime because of man. Build a boat from resinous wood; I am going to cover the earth with a flood, and destroy every living thing... everything in which there is the breath of life. All will die.'

God promised to keep Noah safe in the boat, together with his wife and sons and their wives. He told Noah to bring a pair of every living animal into the boat in order to keep them alive during the flood. 'Bring in a pair of each kind of bird, animal and reptile; store in the boat all the food that you and they will need,' said God; and Noah did everything as God commanded. The day came when God said to Noah, 'Now is the time to go into the boat with all your family.' Then the rains came down in mighty torrents from the sky and the subterranean waters burst forth upon the earth, until finally the waters covered all the high mountains which were under the whole heaven. The waters remained upon the earth for 150 days. All mankind and every living thing upon the face of the earth perished and was blotted out. All was destroyed, leaving only Noah and his family to repopulate the earth. God gave man another chance (Gen.: 6).

The world again is facing the wrath of Almighty God. For those who try to live their lives apart from God, there is only fear and despair to look forward to. Again the world is filled with evil and wicked people. Sin is rampant everywhere. The earth again is filled with crime because of the sins of man. Television has become a gutter through which passes a vast volume of filth. Sex and murder vie with each other for first place. Anyone who finds entertainment through watching such things is actually fellowshipping with the Devil himself. The use of profane language and blasphemy of the Holy Name of Jesus Christ have become acceptable practices.

The explosive interest in the occult is another sign of the times in which we live; in the last days, the Bible teaches, men will turn away from the faith and follow the doctrines of the devil – astrology, fortune-telling, spiritism, yoga, magic and Satanism of every kind, which are objects of abhorrence and disgust to God. God is love, but He is also just and fair. He will not allow sin to go unpunished, unless there is true repentance.

'For God so loved the world, that He gave His only begotten Son, that whosoever believeth in Him should not perish, but have everlasting life' (John 3: 16).

The Word of God, the Holy Bible, was written to rebuke,

150

*correct, instruct and for an example* (2 Timothy 3: 16). *Not one Bible prophecy of the past has failed to be fulfilled. Future prophecies will not fail either. The first most significant fulfilment of Bible prophecy was the birth of our Lord Jesus, as prophesied by Isaiah 700 years before our Lord was born. The second most significant fulfilment of Bible prophecy was the founding of the nation of Israel in 1948 with the subsequent recapture of the old city of Jerusalem by the Jews in 1967. This momentous event, prophesied thousands of years ago, has been fulfilled in our lifetime.*

*During the 1967 Israeli war, 2½ million Jews faced 110 million Arabs. In spite of the odds against her, Israel triumphed over her enemies in less than 100 hours. This was, without doubt, the Lord's doing: the intervening hand of the Lord God, Jehovah. During the past twenty years God has changed the wilderness into a fertile garden. Food, not so long ago, had to be imported to supply Israel's basic needs; now Israel is exporting agricultural goods to many nations throughout the world.*

'But for Israel, good times will return. There will be heavy crops of fruit to prepare for my people's return – and they will be coming home again soon! See, I am for you, and I will come and help you as you prepare the ground and sow your crops. I will greatly increase your population throughout all Israel, and the ruined cities will be rebuilt and filled with people. Not only the people, but your flocks and herds will also greatly multiply. O mountains of Israel, again you will be filled with homes. I will do even more for you than I did before. Then you shall know I am the Lord. My people will walk upon you once again, and you will belong to them again; and you will no longer be a place for burning their children on idol altars' (Ezek. 36: 8–12 LB).

*For the past twenty years, the whole world has been witnessing the return of the Jewish people to the Promised Land and God has been raising up prophets and teachers to tell the world what He is doing for His chosen people.*

*God's time for Israel has come: the time of fulfilment is at hand. To fail to see what the Lord God of Israel is doing in*

*her midst is to have eyes that do not want to see and ears that
do not want to hear. God promised thousands of years ago:*

'Then the LORD thy God will turn thy captivity, and have
compassion upon thee, and will return and gather thee from
all the nations, whither the LORD thy God hath scattered thee.
If any of thine be driven out unto the outmost parts of
heaven, from thence will the LORD thy God gather thee, and
from thence will he fetch thee: and the LORD thy God will
bring thee into the land which thy fathers possessed, and
thou shalt possess it; and He will do thee good, and multiply
thee above thy fathers. And the LORD thy God will circumcise
thine heart, and the heart of thy seed, to love the LORD thy
God with all thine heart, and with all thy soul, that thou
mayest live' (Deut 30: 3-6).

*Today there are still Jews in Russia and in the countries
behind the Iron Curtain. God has spoken to my heart that
the Lord God of Israel is about to open the eyes of the whole
world, and show that He is a living God who KEEPS HIS
WORD. He is going to release His people from the NORTH
COUNTRY; we shall see, in the very near future, hundreds
of thousands of Jews being led out of Russia, through
Poland and Finland, along the highway that God has
prepared.*

'And an highway shall be there, and a way, and it shall be
called the Way of Holiness' (Isa. 35: 8).

*God is preparing for this march now. The Lord has told
believers along that highway to prepare to receive His people
as they come out of Russia and journey home to the
Promised Land. Practical provisions are being made today.*

'Son of dust, when the people of Israel were living in their
own country, they defiled it by their evil deeds; to me their
worship was as foul as filthy rags. They polluted the land
with murder and with the worshipping of idols, so I poured
out my fury upon them. And I exiled them to many lands;
that is how I punished them for the evil way they lived. But
when they were scattered out among the nations, then they
were a blight upon my holy name because the nations said,
"These are the people of God, and he couldn't protect them
from harm!" I am concerned about my reputation that was

ruined by my people throughout the world. Therefore say to the people of Israel: The Lord God says, I am bringing you back again, but not because you deserve it; I am doing it to protect my holy name which you tarnished among the nations. I will honour my great name that you defiled, and the people of the world shall know I am the Lord. I will be honoured before their eyes by delivering you from exile among them. For I will bring you back home again to the land of Israel' (Ezek. 36: 17–24 LB).

'Listen to this message from the Lord, you nations of the world, and publish it abroad: The Lord who scattered His people will gather them back together again and watch over them as a shepherd does his flock' (Jer. 31: 10 LB). 'For I will bring them from the north and from earth's farthest ends, not forgetting their blind and lame, young mothers with their little ones, those ready to give birth. It will be a great company who comes. Tears of joy shall stream down their faces, and I will lead them home with great care. They shall walk beside the quiet streams and not stumble. For I am a Father to Israel, and Ephraim is my oldest child' (Jer. 31: 8–9 LB).

'But there will come a glorious day, says the Lord, when the whole topic of conversation will be that God is bringing his people home from the countries of the north, where he had sent them as slaves for punishment. You will look back no longer to the time I brought you out from slavery in Egypt. That mighty miracle will scarcely be mentioned any more. Yes, I will bring you back again, says the Lord, to this same land I gave your fathers' (Jer. 16: 14–15 LB). 'HE THAT SCATTERED ISRAEL WILL GATHER HIM, AND KEEP HIM, AS A SHEPHERD DOTH HIS FLOCK' (Jer. 31: 10).

'Even the wilderness and desert will rejoice in those days; the desert will blossom with flowers. Yes, there will be an abundance of flowers and singing and joy! The deserts will become as green as the Lebanon mountains, as lovely as Mount Carmel's pastures and Sharon's meadows; for the Lord will display His glory there, the excellency of our God. With this news bring cheer to all discouraged ones.

Encourage those who are afraid. Tell them, 'Be strong, fear not, for your God is coming to destroy your enemies. He is coming to save you.' And when He comes, He will open the eyes of the blind, and unstop the ears of the deaf. The lame man will leap up like a deer, and those who could not speak will shout and sing! Springs will burst forth in the wilderness, and streams in the desert. The parched ground will become a pool, with springs of water in the thirsty land. Where desert jackals lived, there will be reeds and rushes! And a main road will go through that once-deserted land; it will be named "The Holy Highway". No evil-hearted men may walk upon it. God will walk there with you; even the most stupid cannot miss the way. No lion will lurk along its course, nor will there be any other dangers; only the redeemed will travel there. These, the ransomed of the Lord, will go home along that road to Zion, singing the songs of everlasting joy . . .' (Isa. 35: 1–10 LB).

'The Spirit of the Lord God is upon me, because the Lord has anointed me to bring good news to the suffering and afflicted. He has sent me to comfort the broken-hearted, to announce liberty to captives and to open the eyes of the blind. He has sent me to tell those who mourn that the time of God's favour to them has come, and the day of His wrath to their enemies. To all who mourn in Israel He will give:

> Beauty for ashes;
> Joy instead of mourning;
> Praise instead of heaviness.

For God has planted them like strong and graceful oaks for His own glory.

'And they shall rebuild the ancient ruins, repairing cities long ago destroyed, reviving them though they have lain there many generations. Foreigners shall be your servants; they shall feed your flocks and plough your fields and tend your vineyards. You shall be called priests of the Lord, ministers of our God. You shall be fed with the treasures of the nations and shall glory in their riches. Instead of shame and dishonour, you shall have a double portion of prosperity and everlasting joy. For I, the Lord, love justice; I hate robbery and wrong. I will faithfully reward my people for their suffering and make an everlasting covenant with them. Their descendants shall be known and honoured among the nations; all shall realise that they are a people God has blessed . . . The Lord will show the nations of the world His justice; all will praise Him. His righteousness shall be like a budding tree, or like a garden in early spring, full of young plants springing up everywhere' (Isa. 61: 1–9, 11 LB).

'O Jerusalem, I have set intercessors on your walls who shall cry to God all day and all night for the fulfilment of His promises. Take no rest, all you who pray, and give God no rest until He establishes Jerusalem and makes her respected and admired throughout the earth' (Isa. 62: 6–7 LB). 'See the Lord has sent His messengers to every land and said, 'Tell my people, I, the Lord your God, am coming to save you and will bring you many gifts." And they shall be called "The Holy People" and "The Lord's Redeemed", and Jerusalem shall be called "The Land of Desire" and "The City God has Blessed"' (Isa. 62: 11–12 LB). 'Don't be afraid, for I am with you. I will gather you from east and west, from north and south. I will bring my sons and daughters back to Israel from the farthest corners of the earth' (Isa. 43: 5-6 LB).

*The Lord God, Jehovah, is coming to SAVE his people. I cannot see to write: my eyes are full of tears: the anointing of the Lord is strong upon me. Cry out to the Lord, all ye people of the nations of the world: release your people, O God, from the Country of the NORTH. Cry out in the Spirit, all ye his people. Take no rest, all you who pray – cry to God, all day and all night! Give God no rest until He releases His children, who are at present being held captive, suffering great hardship and persecution in the Country of the North.*

## ANOTHER EXODUS

'"Now you will see that I shall do to Pharaoh,"' the Lord told Moses. "For he must be forced to let my people go; he will not only let them go, but will *drive them out of his land!* I am

155

Jehovah, the Almighty God who appeared to Abraham, Isaac and Jacob – though I did not reveal my name, Jehovah, to them. And I entered into a solemn covenant with them; under its terms I promised to give them and their descendants the land of Canaan where they were living. And now I have heard the groanings of the people of Israel, in slavery now to the Egyptians, and I remember my promise. Therefore tell the descendants of Israel that I will use my mighty power and perform great miracles to deliver them from slavery, and make them free."' (Exod. 6: 1–6 LB)

*Remember the first Exodus. God showed His commitment to His chosen people by sparing them from the plagues which came upon the land of Egypt, and delivering them out of the hand of Pharaoh when every first-born son of the Egyptians had been struck dead. By His great power alone, He led them to the banks of the Red Sea, and stretched out His hand to work a mighty miracle even when their hearts were almost failing them for fear:*

'But Moses told the people, "Don't be afraid. Just stand where you are and watch, and you will see the wonderful way the Lord will rescue you today. The Egyptians you are looking at – you will never see them again. The Lord will fight for you, and you won't need to lift a finger!" Then the Lord said to Moses, "Stop praying and get the people moving! Forward, march! Use your rod – hold it out over the water, and the sea will open up a path before you, and all the people of Israel shall walk through on dry ground! I will harden the hearts of the Egyptians and they will go in after you and you will see the honour I will get in defeating Pharaoh and all his armies, chariots, and horsemen. And all Egypt shall know that I am Jehovah."

'Then the Angel of God, who was leading the people of Israel, moved the cloud round behind them, and it stood between the people of Israel and the Egyptians. And that night, as it changed to a pillar of fire, it gave darkness to the Egyptians but light to the people of Israel! So the Egyptians couldn't find the Israelites! Meanwhile, Moses stretched his rod over the sea, and the Lord opened up a path through the sea, with walls of water on each side; and a strong east wind blew all that night, drying the sea bottom. So the people of Israel walked through the sea on dry ground!

'Then the Egyptians followed them between the walls of water along the bottom of the sea – all of Pharaoh's horses, chariots and horsemen. But in the early morning, Jehovah looked down from the cloud of fire upon the array of the Egyptians and began to harass them. Their chariot wheels began coming off, so that their chariots scraped along the dry ground. "Let's get out of here," the Egyptians yelled. "Jehovah is fighting for them and against us." When all the Israelites were on the other side, the Lord said to Moses, "Stretch out your hand again over the sea, so that the waters will come back over the Egyptians, and their chariots and horsemen." Moses did, and the sea returned to normal beneath the morning light. The Egyptians tried to flee, but the Lord drowned them in the sea. The water covered the path and the chariots and horsemen. And of all the army of Pharaoh that chased after Israel through the sea, not one remained alive. The people of Israel had walked through on dry land, and the waters had been walled up on either side of them. Thus Jehovah saved Israel that day from the Egyptians; and the people of Israel saw the Egyptians dead, washed up on the seashore. When the people of Israel saw the mighty miracle the Lord had done for them against the Egyptians, they were afraid and revered the Lord, and believed in him and in his servant Moses' (Exod. 14: 13–31 LB).

*We shall see an Exodus of even greater magnitude in our lifetime. The Lord God of Israel will show Himself to be a faithful God who never changes and all the world will wonder at His power. It is my belief that God will raise up people with ministries like those of Moses and Aaron. They will go forth and perform mighty miracles in the name of Jesus, and demand that the Country of the North release the children of Israel. I asked the Lord to give me confirmation of this from His Word:*

'"Yes," replies the Lord, "I will do mighty miracles for you, like those when I brought you out of slavery in Egypt. All the world will stand amazed at what I will do for you, and be embarrassed by their puny might. They will stand in silent awe, deaf to all around them. They will see what snakes they are, lowly as worms crawling from their holes. They will come trembling out of their fortresses to meet the Lord our God. They will fear him; they will stand in awe'' (Mic. 7: 15–17 LB). 'And the Lord said, "Blessed is she that believed: for there shall be a performance of those things which were told her from the Lord"' (Luke 1: 45).

*Once God's promise is fulfilled and He had brought all His children home from the Country of the North to the Promised Land, they will then build the temple and begin to perform their sacrifices and offerings to God. During that time they will make a seven-year peace treaty with a powerful man who is gaining world control. This powerful leader will guarantee them freedom of worship and promise them safety. The Jewish people will live in peace for only the first three and a half years of this treaty. This powerful leader will reveal himself to be none other than the Antichrist. He will break his peace covenant with the children of Israel, stop them making their sacrifices to God, set up an image of himself in the Jewish Temple and proclaim that he, himself, is God. At that time he will join forces with the King of the North. As the Egyptians pursued the children of Israel with the intention of destroying them and bringing the survivors again into slavery, so will Russia and the nations under the rule of the Antichrist come against Jerusalem with the intention of utterly destroying her for ever, in the great battle of Armageddon. As the Egyptians pursued Israel only days after their release from Egypt, so, I believe, the events of the Antichrist and the end of this world order will happen in quick succession after the children of Israel have returned to the Promised Land from the Country of the North.*

## CASHLESS SOCIETY

*The third most significant fulfilment of Bible prophecy of this age is the development and implementation of the '666' system, as prophesied in the Book of Revelation.*

'And he causeth all, both small and great, rich and poor, free and bond, to receive a mark in their right hand, or in their foreheads: and that no man might buy or sell, save he that had the mark, or the name of the beast, or the number of his name. Here is wisdom. Let him that hath understanding count the number of the beast: for it is the number of a man; and his number is Six hundred threescore and six' (Rev. 13: 16–18) . . . '666' . . .!

*Scripture is being fulfilled, even as you sit here and read at this moment. You and I are already part of, and using, this '666' system. I believe that we are the generation that will see the Second Coming of Jesus Christ. We shall see Jesus coming in the clouds of heaven in power and great glory, to save His true Church before the destruction and wrath of God which is coming upon the earth. The beast referred to in the scripture (Rev. 13: 17–18) is the Antichrist, the son of hell, therefore the number, '666' is his. Is it just coincidence that the number 666 has been appearing in many countries throughout the world, stamped upon products, inscribed in seals, and is now part of the identifying number on many national and international credit cards? Also many computers all over the world have their transactions prefixed with the number '666'.*

*During 1982–3 articles appeared in business journals and the national press concerning the introduction of automated payment-systems (Electronic Fund Transfer – EFT) to meet customers' needs. These include slot-card payments at petrol pumps, a system of selling petrol by instantly debiting the driver's bank account, and cash-free shopping schemes devised by banks and supermarkets to get customers to pay their bills with 'plastics' Rummaging in your purse for cash or paying by cheque at the supermarket will soon be a thing of the past. Motorists wishing to park in a large section of Inner London will soon be faced with a new-style meter, which will accept only plastic cards. These are but a few of the latest steps towards a cashless society.*

*During the months of July and August 1981, the Inland Revenue Service in America made a grave mistake; but this mistake was in accordance with the will of God, Hallelujah! God never makes mistakes. Several states in America, such as Kentucky, Indiana, Maryland and Virginia confirmed the startling news. It seemed that social security cheques, requiring a special and unusual process for cashing, were accidentally mailed to recipients. A paragraph with instructions and requirements for cashing government cheques is printed on the back. It formally states that proper identification must be shown at the time when the cheque is being endorsed for cashing.*

*The instructional paragraph on these particular cheques read that the party cashing the cheque must have the proper identification 'MARK' in the right hand or in the forehead. Without this, the cheque could not be cashed. The banks as well as the recipients were surprised, confused and frustrated. In spite of all demands, the banks refused to cash any of the cheques. After much confusion, denials and argument the Inland Revenue Service admitted its mistake. The cheques were valid social security cheques. However, they were not usable . . . the problem with them was that they had been issued too soon. The government cheques, requiring a 'MARK' in the right hand or in the forehead, are not to be brought into use until a later date, but they are ready and waiting to be sent out, when the time is right. So many people are dependent upon the Government and private business organisations for unemployment and social security benefits, or mortgages and loan/credit facilities, they are caught in a cleft stick. God supplies all my needs: He can supply yours, if you trust Him, too!*

*The most gigantic computer complex in the world is located in Luxembourg. Through the use of credit cards, information about trading nations has been fed into that memory bank. You and I are tied into that computer. Every move that you make, every penny that you pay in taxes is all on record. Your identity number is already on record in that computer.*

*The world is about to merge into what will be known as a cashless society; it is as difficult for us to imagine a world without cash as it was for our parents to believe that man*

160

would go to the moon. Man did go to the moon: we are on the verge of the total elimination of all monies in the world. A new world exchange system is imminent: all buying and selling will be conducted by means of a single PLASTIC DEBIT CARD.

It is only a matter of time – and the time is short – when every person on the face of the earth will be assigned an identity mark, which will be laser-beamed into the right hand or into the forehead. Let's go back to the scripture: 'And no man might buy or sell, save he that had the mark, or the name of the beast, or the number of his name' (Rev. 13: 17). We know that the number of the beast is '666': I believe that the 'mark' of the beast is the set of vertical markings which appears on containers or wrappings of most manufactured products nowadays.

Although these markings mean little to the naked eye, check-out computers scan them with an electronic eye, which translates them into meaningful information about the product, where it came from, how many items came into stock, and so on; but it is not only for stock control . . . it is also part of the new One World Government System. It is my belief that people throughout the world will be faced with the decision of having the mark placed in the right hand or on the forehead. As in the case of the vertical markings on product wrappings and containers, the scanners will be able to obtain all necessary information and personal details of identification from the mark, which will have become part of the human body. The process of placing the mark in the human body will be painless, and the mark will be invisible to the naked eye; but it will be as permanent and unique as one's finger-prints.

# How Near Is It?

*It will begin when everyone is issued with a debit card. All commerce and trade will be conducted by means of a single debit card. People will be paid by computer directly into their personal bank accounts. The debit card will be used in retail stores; it will be used for all monetary transactions, including the payment of bills, and even when applying for a mortgage advance. Instead of going to a supermarket, with cash in a purse, one will need only the debit card, which will be scanned and processed by the electronic eye and the computer, in order to obtain all the information it requires about the debit-card holder.*

*The amount just spent in the store will be deducted immediately and automatically from one's personal bank account by means of the computer: no cash, no change, no cheques. The advantage of a cashless society would be enormous: much crime would be eliminated, and it would seem to be the answer to the world's problem of ridding society of muggings and robberies. The Devil is so subtle. For those who have ears to hear, listen to what the Holy Spirit is saying to the Church. These debit cards will be the means through which the mark of the beast will be introduced into the world. The next step is that the identity mark will become part of the human body: it will be put into the right hand or the forehead, and become a permanent personal record.*

## WARNING: WHOSOEVER RECEIVES THE MARK OF THE BEAST . . .

'And the third angel followed them, saying with a loud voice,

If any man worship the beast and his image, and receive his mark in his forehead, or in his hand, the same shall drink of the wine of the wrath of God, which is poured out without mixture into the cup of His indignation; and he shall be tormented with fire and brimstone in the presence of the holy angels, and in the presence of the Lamb: and the smoke of their torment ascendeth up for ever and ever: and they have no rest day nor night, who worship the beast and his image, and whosoever receiveth the mark of his name. Here is the patience of the saints: here are they that keep the commandments of God, and the faith of Jesus. And I heard a voice from heaven saying unto me, Write, Blessed are the dead which die in the Lord from henceforth: Yea, saith the Spirit, that they may rest from their labours; and their works do follow them' (Rev. 14: 9–13).

*ANYONE who has the mark or number put in the right hand or forehead will be for ever doomed to spend eternity in the flames of eternal perdition. Whosoever receives the mark will NOT inherit the Kingdom of God. God's word will change for no man. God's word will never change.* 'Heaven and earth shall pass away, but my words shall not pass away' (Matt. 24: 35).

'And as Jesus sat upon the mount of Olives, the disciples came unto Him privately, saying, Tell us, when shall these things be? and what shall be the sign of thy coming, and of the end of the world? And Jesus answered and said unto them, Take heed that no man deceived you. For many shall come in my name, saying, I am Christ; and shall deceive many.

'And ye shall hear of wars and rumours of wars: see that ye be not troubled: for all these things must come to pass, but the end is not yet. For nation shall rise against nation, and kingdom against kingdom: and there shall be famines, and pestilences, and earthquakes, in divers places. All these are the beginning of sorrows. Then shall they deliver you up to be afflicted, and shall kill you: and ye shall be hated of all nations for my name's sake' (Matt. 24: 3–9). *Jesus said that Christians would be tortured and killed all over the world* 'FOR MY NAME'S SAKE'. *He is not talking about the*

*Jews here: they have not at this point received Jesus as their Messiah.*

'And then shall many be offended, and shall betray one another, and shall hate one another' (Matt. 24: 10). *Many people who are professing to be Christians, but are not 'born again', will betray and hate one another.* 'And many false prophets shall rise, and shall deceive many. And because iniquity shall abound, the love of many shall wax cold' (Matt. 24: 11–12). *Sin will be rampant everywhere, and cool the love of many.* 'But he that shall endure until the end, the same shall be saved. And this gospel of the kingdom shall be preached in all the world for a witness unto all nations; and then shall the end come' (Matt. 24: 13–14). 'Then if any man shall say unto you, Lo, here is Christ, or there: believe it not' (Matt. 24: 23).

*In August 1982, a man spent £200,000 proclaiming that the Christ would appear within two months. This was advertised in the press of fourteen different countries throughout the world. This man was one of the false prophets of whom our Lord warned us.*

'For there shall arise false Christs, and false prophets, and shall shew forth great signs and wonders; insomuch that, if it were possible, they shall deceive the very elect' (Matt. 24: 24).

*The Antichrist and False Prophet will perform wonderful miracles using satanic power. These miracles will be so convincing that they could deceive even the born-again. Praise God, it will not be possible to deceive us if we truly know Him and are led by the Holy Spirit.*

'Behold, I have told you before. Wherefore if they shall say unto you, Behold, he is in the desert; go not forth: behold, he is in the secret chambers; believe it not. For as the lightning cometh out of the east, and shineth even unto the west; so shall also the coming of the Son of man be. For wheresoever the carcase is, there will the eagles be gathered together' (Matt. 24: 25–8).

*There will be no doubt in anyone's mind when the Lord Jesus comes back for His Bride: as the lightning flashes across the sky, so Christ will appear in the clouds of heaven in great glory.*

'Now learn a parable of the fig-tree; when his branch is yet tender, and putteth forth leaves, ye know that summer is nigh: so likewise ye, when ye shall see all these things, know that it is near, even at the doors. Verily I say unto you, this generation shall not pass, till all these things be fulfilled' (Matt. 24: 32–4).

*When the trees begin to bud and bring forth their leaves, you know in your heart that summer is near. So there will be wars and rumours of wars, earthquakes and famines; and when you see the evidence of the rise of the Antichrist, you will know in your heart that this will be the generation that will see Jesus coming in the clouds of heaven.*

'Heaven and earth shall pass away, but my words shall not pass away' (Matt. 24: 35). *Heaven and earth shall pass away indeed: God is planning to burn up this earth and provide us with a beautiful new world. His word shall remain for ever.*

*The Lord fed the children of Israel with manna from heaven during the forty years they were in the wilderness. In the evening, the Lord fed them with meat: vast numbers of quail arrived and covered the camp. In the morning, the Lord fed them with bread: it was white and flat and tasted like honey. The time is coming when we won't be able to buy food. Those who have faith to receive, the Lord will feed with manna from heaven. Hallelujah!*

'He that hath an ear, let him hear what the Spirit saith unto the churches: To him that overcometh will I give to eat of the hidden manna, and will give him a white stone, and in the stone a new name written, which no man knoweth saving he that receiveth it' (Rev. 2: 17).


## ANTICHRIST

*We shall see the rise of a super world-dictator who will gain control over all the nations (Rev. 13: 7). The world will come under one government. Aligned with this world ruler will be the False Prophet (Rev. 19: 20; 20: 10), the second Beast of Revelation 13: 11, who will be head of a one-world church, called Babylon in Scripture* (Rev. 17: 5). *This church will be formed by the merging of all religious denominations and sects throughout the world, people of all kindreds, tongues and nations.*

The Antichrist will be a man of unprecedented wickedness and will gain power through cunning and deception, using flatteries to attain his ends. There will also be an element of mystery about him; he will manifest a preternatural power which he will receive from Satan, the Devil. By means of this satanic power, he will deceive the masses and draw their admiration and praise.

Initially the Antichrist will feign friendship with the officially approved 'Church', waiting only for the time when his power has been strengthened. The False Prophet will work great signs and wonders in his name, and by concealing his true identity the Antichrist will appear the answer to all the world's problems. This brilliant politician will make a seven-year peace treaty with the Jewish people (Dan. 9: 27). Multitudes will fall for this deception because of their ignorance of the Word of God. The world will be so intrigued by his words that they will believe all he says about peace and safety (1 Thess. 5: 3).

But having lulled everyone into a false sense of security and trust, the Antichrist will begin to enforce his rulership upon the world. It will become obvious that his aim is to eliminate all Christians, and afterwards Jews, from the face of the earth. After many of those who are truly born again of the Spirit of God have been liquidated, he will turn his attention to the church he had feigned to favour. All those who continue to profess Jesus Christ and oppose the doctrine of this apostate church may also face the fate of the martyrs. This persecution forms the Great Tribulation and lasts for three and a half years.

Striking at their most vulnerable point – families must have food in order to live – the son of hell will issue a decree that no man may buy or sell unless he has an identification mark in his forehead or in his right hand. This cruel decree will begin the most terrible persecution the world has ever known. Many Christians will be faced with the terrible

166

*dilemma – to take the mark of Satan, or be beheaded.*

'Then the Dragon encouraged the Creature to speak great blasphemies against the Lord; and gave him authority to control the earth for forty-two months. All that time he blasphemed God's Name and his temple and all those living in heaven. The Dragon gave him power to fight against God's people and to overcome them, and to rule over all nations and language groups throughout the world. And all mankind – whose names were not written down before the founding of the world in the slain Lamb's Book of Life – worshipped the evil Creature. Anyone who can hear, listen carefully. The people of God who are destined for prison will be arrested and taken away; those destined for death will be killed. But do not be dismayed, for here is your opportunity for endurance and confidence' (Rev. 13: 5–10). *Be ye faithful unto death.*

'He [the Antichrist] will defy the Most High God, and wear down the saints with persecution, and try to change all laws, morals and customs. God's people will be helpless in his hands for three and a half years' (Dan. 7: 25 LB).

'Then you will be tortured and killed and hated all over the world because you are mine, and many of you shall fall back into sin and betray and hate each other. And many false prophets will appear and lead many astray' (Matt. 24: 9–11 LB).

'And when he had opened the fifth seal, I saw under the altar the souls of them that were slain for the Word of God, and for the testimony which they held: And they cried with a loud voice, saying, How long, O Lord, holy and true, dost thou not judge and avenge our blood on them that dwell on earth? And white robes were given unto every one of them, that they should rest yet for a little season, UNTIL THEIR FELLOW SERVANTS ALSO AND THEIR BRETHREN, THAT SHOULD BE KILLED AS THEY WERE, SHOULD BE FULFILLED' (Rev. 6: 9–11).

*God showed John in a vision things that would come to pass, and he saw the souls of those beheaded for the witness of Jesus and the Word of God.*

'These people had not worshipped the beast or his image,

neither had they received the mark in the right hand or in the forehead. They lived and reigned with Christ for a thousand years' (Rev. 20: 4 LB).

*Midway through his reign, the Antichrist will suffer a fatal wound and will be killed. He will actually come back to life for the remaining three and a half years of this dispensation.* 'And I saw one of his heads as it were wounded to death; and his deadly wound was healed: and all the world wondered after the beast. And they worshipped the dragon which gave power unto the beast, saying, Who is like unto the beast? who is able to make war with him?' (Rev. 13: 3–4). 'The beast that thou sawest was, and is not; and shall ascend out of the bottomless pit, and go into perdition: and they that dwell on the earth shall wonder, whose names were not written in the book of life from the foundation of the world, when they behold the beast that was, and is not, and yet is' (Rev. 17: 8).

*He will ascend out of the pit of hell, and be totally controlled and dominated by Satan, revealing himself as Satan's masterpiece, utterly anti-Christ and anti-God. He will break his peace treaty with the Jews* (Dan. 9: 27) *and subject them to the same persecution as the Christians. He will take away all their freedom of worship and set himself up as God in the temple of Jerusalem* (2 Thess. 2: 4), *demanding the adoration and worship of all the people of the nations under his rule.*

'When ye therefore shall see the abomination of desolation, spoken of by Daniel the prophet, stand in the holy place, (whoso readeth, let him understand:)' (Matt. 24: 15). *The abomination of desolation is when the Antichrist sits in the temple of God, and proclaims that he, himself, is God.* 'Then let them which be in Judaea flee into the mountains' (Matt. 24: 16). *The Jews at this time must flee into the mountains.*

'Let him which is on the housetop not come down to take anything out of his house: neither let him which is in the field return back to take his clothes. And woe unto them that are with child, and to them that give suck in those days!' (Matt. 24: 17–19).

The Jews will have to give up the security of homes and hospitals. Pregnant women will suffer extreme hardship at this time; babies will have to be born in caves in mountains. Because of lack of food, mothers' milk supplies will be very poor, and they will fear for the lives of their suckling babies.

'But pray ye that your flight be not in the winter, neither on the sabbath day:' (Matt. 24: 20) for then shall be great tribulation, such as was not since the beginning of the world to this time, no, nor ever shall be. And except those days should be shortened, there should no flesh be saved: but for the elect's sake those days shall be shortened' (Matt. 24: 20-2).

It would be extremely cold up in the mountains during the winter months with no form of heating. All flesh would perish, but for the sake of the Jews and born-again saints of God, the time will be cut short.

The Bride of Christ and the Jewish race will face persecution such as was not since the beginning of the world to this time, no nor ever shall be. Jesus warned, 'if they persecuted me they shall persecute you: whosoever shall save his life shall lose it, and whosoever shall lose his life for my sake shall find it.'

'Let no man deceive you by any means: for that day shall not come, except there come a falling away first, and that man of sin be revealed, the son of perdition; Who opposeth and exalteth himself above all that is called God, or that is worshipped; so that he as God sitteth in the temple of God, shewing himself that he is God. Remember ye not, that, when I was yet with you, I told you these things?' (2 Thess. 2: 3-5).

The falling away will be when people, professing Christianity, but not born again, will turn from the faith and receive the identifying mark of Satan. Scripture states that the man of sin, the Antichrist, will be revealed before the Lord returns for His Bride. Praise God! Death to the true Christian is to be with Jesus for eternity: never to die again. Because Jesus rose from the dead, we also shall rise from the dead and live for ever.

'FOR TO ME TO LIVE IS CHRIST, AND TO DIE IS GAIN' (Phil. 1: 21).

# The Rapture

## JESUS RETURNS AND PUTS AN END TO THE PERSECUTION OF HIS PEOPLE

*Jesus Christ, who rose from the dead and now lives for ever, will appear in only one way – that is, in the clouds of heaven with power and great glory. As the lightning flashes across the sky from east to west, so shall the coming of the Son of man be. There is no greater certainty. He will not need television to announce his coming: the very heavens and earth will shake with the mighty power of God when Jesus comes to collect His Bride, the true Church. Jesus will draw His own people to Himself through the Holy Spirit that is within them. In the twinkling of an eye, as quickly as it takes to blink, our earthly bodies will be changed and we shall receive our new immortal bodies, which will never grow old and never die.*

'Immediately after the tribulation of those days shall the sun be darkened, and the moon shall not give her light, and the stars shall fall from heaven, and the powers of the heavens shall be shaken: and then shall appear the sign of the Son of man in heaven: and then shall all the tribes of the earth mourn, and they shall see the Son of man coming in the clouds of heaven with power and great glory' (Matt. 24: 29–30).

*The Lord Jesus will put an end to the tribulation of the saints with His appearing in the clouds.* 'And He shall send His angels with a great sound of a trumpet, and they shall gather together His elect from the four winds, from one end of heaven to the other' (Matt. 24: 31).

*The last trumpet will sound, and all born-again believers*

170

*who are still alive on earth will experience the miracle of the rapture. They will not see death: the earthly body will be changed into an immortal body, and instantly be translated to heaven.*

'For the Lord Himself shall descend from heaven with a shout, and with the voice of the archangel, and with the trump of God: and the dead in Christ shall rise first: then we which are alive and remain shall be caught up together with them in the clouds, to meet the Lord in the air: and so shall we ever be with the Lord. Wherefore comfort one another with these words' (1 Thess. 4: 16–18).

'I tell you this, my brothers: an earthly body made of flesh and blood cannot get into God's kingdom. These perishable bodies of ours are not the right kind to live for ever. But I am telling you this strange and wonderful secret: we shall not all die, but we shall all be given new bodies! It will all happen in a moment, in the twinkling of an eye, when the last trumpet is blown. For there will be a trumpet blast from the sky, and all the Christians who have died will suddenly come alive with new bodies that will never, never die; and then we who are still alive shall suddenly have new bodies too. For our earthly bodies, the ones we have now that can die, must be transformed into heavenly bodies that cannot perish but will live for ever' (1 Cor. 15: 50–3 LB).

'But of that day and hour knoweth no man, no, not the angels of heaven, but my Father only. But as the days of Noe were, so shall also the coming of the Son of man be. For as in the days that were before the flood they were eating and drinking, marrying and giving in marriage, until the day that Noe entered into the ark, and knew not until the flood came, and took them all away; so shall also the coming of the Son of man be' (Matt. 24: 36–9).

*The people living on the earth in Noah's day would not repent of their sins and listen to Noah. 'Look at him building that boat; he thinks he is in touch with God,' they laughed, and continued life in their normal, sinful way, as though nothing would happen. Then the floods came and destroyed them. It will be just the same when the Lord returns: the people of the world will be living normal, sinful lives.*

'Then shall two be in the field; the one shall be taken, and the other left. Two women shall be grinding at the mill; the one shall be taken, and the other left' (Matt. 24: 40–1).

*All who are born of the spirit of God will be caught up to heaven. The heathen will be left on earth to face the wrath of Almighty God. Noah and his family were taken from the earth and placed in the safety of the boat. Then the flood came and destroyed all the sinful inhabitants of the earth. So it will be when the Lord returns; He will translate His Bride to heaven, then the wrath of God will come upon the inhabitants of the earth.*

'Watch therefore: for ye know not at what hour your Lord doth come. But know this, that if the goodman of the house had known in what watch the thief would come, he would have watched, and would not have suffered his house to be broken up. Therefore be ye also ready: for in such an hour as ye think not the Son of man cometh' (Matt. 24: 42–4).


## THE BRIDE OF CHRIST IN HEAVEN – THE MARRIAGE FEAST OF THE LAMB

*During the next three and a half years God will pour out His wrath upon the Antichrist, the False Prophet and all his followers, during which time the Bride of Christ is safely in heaven. All who have been raised at the rapture of the Church, both Christians and Old Testament saints, will attend the glorious Marriage Feast of the Lamb. They will be given fine white robes in reward for their righteous deeds and faithfulness, and power and authority will be delegated to them to reign with Christ on the earth for a thousand years.*

'And after these things I heard a great voice of much people in heaven, saying, Alleluia; salvation and glory, and honour and power unto the Lord our God; for true and righteous are his judgments: for he hath judged the great whore, which did corrupt the earth with her fornication, and hath avenged the blood of his servants at her hand. And again they said, Alleluia. And her smoke arose up for ever

172

and ever. And the four and twenty elders and the four beasts fell down and worshipped God that sat upon the throne, saying, Amen; Alleluia. And a voice came out of the throne saying, Praise our God, all ye His servants, and ye that fear Him, both small and great. And I heard as it were the voice of a great multitude, and as the voice of many waters, and as the voice of mighty thunderings, saying, Alleluia, for the Lord God omnipotent reigneth. Let us be glad and rejoice, and give honour to Him: for the marriage of the Lamb is come, and His wife hath made herself ready. And to her was granted that she should be arrayed in fine linen, clean and white; for the fine linen is the righteousness of the saints. And he saith unto me, Write, Blessed are they which are called unto the marriage supper of the Lamb. And he saith unto me, These are the true sayings of God' (Rev. 19: 1–9).

*The Word of God never fails: these scriptures will be fulfilled. We shall see these things come to pass. God's people will be clothed in robes of righteousness, singing 'Praise the Lord, for the Lord, our God the Almighty reigns!' Yes, what a day that will be, and blessed are those who have prepared themselves for the Wedding Feast of the Lamb.*

'After this I beheld, and, lo, a great multitude, which no man could number, of all nations, and kindreds, and people, and tongues, stood before the throne, and before the Lamb, clothed with white robes, and palms in their hands; And cried with a loud voice, saying, Salvation to our God which sitteth upon the throne, and unto the Lamb. And all the angels stood round about the throne, and about the elders and the four beasts, and fell before the throne on their faces, and worshipped God, saying, Amen: Blessing, and glory, and wisdom, and thanksgiving, and honour, and power, and might, be unto our God for ever and ever. Amen. And one of the elders answered, saying unto me, What are these that are arrayed in white robes? and whence came they? And I said unto him, Sir, thou knowest. And he said to me, These are they which came out of great tribulation, and have washed their robes, and made them white in the blood of the Lamb. Therefore are they before the throne of God, and serve Him day and night in His temple: and He that sitteth on the throne shall dwell among them. They shall hunger no more, neither thirst any more; neither shall the sun light on them, nor any heat. For the Lamb which is in the midst of the throne shall feed them, and shall lead them unto living fountains of water: and God shall wipe away all tears from their eyes' (Rev. 7: 9–17).

'And I saw as it were a sea of glass mingled with fire: and them that had gotten the victory over the beast, and over his image, and over the number of his name, stand on the sea of glass, having the harps of God. And they sing the song of Moses the servant of God, and the song of the Lamb, saying, Great and marvellous are thy works, Lord God Almighty; just and true are thy ways, thou King of saints. Who shall fear thee, O Lord and glorify thy name? For thou only art holy: for all nations shall come and worship before thee; for thy judgments are made manifest' (Rev. 15: 2–4).

'And he that overcometh, and keepeth my works unto the end, to him will I give power over the nations, and he shall rule them with a rod of iron; as the vessels of a potter shall they be broken to shivers, even as I received of my Father' (Rev. 2: 26–7).

## God's Wrath

## THE LAST THREE AND A HALF YEARS
## OF THIS AGE

*The Great Tribulation, the persecution of God's people, is
satanic, and caused by the son of hell. The Wrath of God is
entirely an affliction from God himself. God will pour out
his anger upon the Beast and the False Prophet who
murdered and killed the Christians and upon all those who
received the mark of the Evil One. The word 'tribulation'
does not appear in Scripture after Revelation 7:14, when the
saints are now in heaven. The Wrath of God then takes over.
But before God gives the command to pour out the vials
upon the earth, he says:*

'Hurt not the earth, neither the sea, nor the trees, till
we have sealed the servants of our God in their foreheads.
And I heard the number of them which were sealed: and
there were sealed an hundred and forty and four thousand of
all the tribes of the children of Israel' (Rev. 7: 3–4).

*God has used the Jews as an example to show all the
nations of the world what will happen to those nations that
reject God, for the Jewish race has been the most persecuted
in all of mankind. God in His love and mercy has promised to
watch over those who are faithful to Him, and of this
number 144,000 will be especially sealed. The 144,000, not
being part of the Church, will be left on earth to go through
the Wrath of God, but will remain unharmed. As it was in
Egypt at the time of the Passover, when the destroying
angels did not harm those protected by blood on their door-
lintels – so also the angels pouring out the wrath of God will
pass over the 144,000 Jews sealed with the seal of God. God*

*also makes further provision for His chosen people to repent and be saved at this time.*

## THE TWO WITNESSES – MOSES AND ELIJAH

'Behold, I will send you Elijah the prophet before the coming of the great and dreadful day of the Lord; and he shall turn the heart of the fathers to the children, and the heart of the children to their fathers, lest I come and smite the earth with a curse' (Mal. 4: 5–6; see also Matt. 17: 1–8).

'And I will give power unto my two witnesses, and they shall prophesy a thousand two hundred and threescore days, clothed in sackcloth. These are the two olive trees, and the two candlesticks standing before the God of the earth. And if any man will hurt them, fire proceedeth out of their mouth, and devoureth their enemies: and if any man will hurt them, he must in this manner be killed. These have power to shut heaven, that it rain not in the days of their prophecy: and have power over waters to turn them to blood, and to smite the earth with all plagues, as often as they will. And when they shall have finished their testimony, the beast that ascendeth out of the bottomless pit shall make war against them, and shall overcome them, and kill them. And their dead bodies shall lie in the street of the great city, which spiritually is called Sodom and Egypt, where also our Lord was crucified. And they of the people and kindreds and tongues and nations shall see their dead bodies three days and an half, and shall not suffer their dead bodies to be put in graves. And they that dwell upon the earth shall rejoice over them, and make merry, and shall send gifts one to another; because these two prophets tormented them that dwelt on the earth. And after three days and an half the Spirit of life from God entered into them, and they stood upon their feet; and great fear fell upon them which saw them. And they heard a great voice from heaven saying unto them, Come up hither. And they ascended up to heaven in a cloud; and their enemies beheld them' (Rev. 11: 3–12).

The ministry of the two witnesses will continue during the last three and a half years of the reign of this world order, during the Wrath of God. They will stand in the streets of Jerusalem, and boldly defy both the Antichrist and the False Prophet. They will proclaim to the nation of Israel that judgment is at hand. Moses and Elijah will declare to the Jewish people that Jesus of Nazareth is their true Messiah, the Lord of heaven and earth. They will urge the Jewish people to repent and accept Jesus as their personal Saviour; they will also warn God's people to have nothing to do with the identifying mark which the Beast has been giving to all those who accept his claims. The two witnesses will boldly proclaim that if anyone worship the Beast or his image, he will be under the penalty of everlasting damnation. The full number of the Gentiles will have come in with the rapture of the Church, and God will use His two witnesses to open the eyes of his people and turn their hearts back to Him. At that time the Lord will pour upon the house of David and all the inhabitants of Jerusalem the Spirit of grace and supplication.

When their ministry has been fulfilled, God will allow the two witnesses to be slain in the streets of Jerusalem. The Antichrist, False Prophet and all their followers will rejoice at the death of these true prophets: their dead bodies will lie on the street, and no one will even attempt to bury them. Praise God! His plans are always perfect; after three and a half days the Spirit of life enters the dead bodies, and the voice of Almighty God calls, 'Come up hither'. The two witnesses will ascend up to heaven in a cloud, as their enemies stand and watch. At that very hour there will be a severe earthquake; seven thousand people will be killed, and the terrified survivors will give glory to the God of heaven. (Rev. 11: 13 LB).

But for the rest of the inhabitants of the earth, it is the time of God's wrath and who will be able to stand?

# WOE, WOE, WOE, TO THE INHABITERS OF THE EARTH

'"You are just in sending this judgment, O Holy One, who is and was, for your saints and prophets have been martyred and their blood poured out upon the earth; and now, in turn, you have poured out the blood of those who murdered them; it is their just reward." And I heard the angel of the altar say, "Yes, Lord God Almighty, your punishments are just and true"' (Rev. 16: 5–7 LB).

'And I beheld when he had opened the sixth seal, and, lo, there was a great earthquake; and the sun became black as sackcloth of hair, and the moon became as blood; and the stars of heaven fell unto the earth, even as a fig tree casteth her untimely figs, when she is shaken of a mighty wind. And the heaven departed as a scroll when it is rolled together; and every mountain and island were moved out of their places. And the kings of the earth and the rich men, and the chief captains, and the mighty men, and every bondman, and every free man, hid themselves in the dens and in the rocks of the mountains; and said to the mountains, Fall on us, and hide us from the face of him that sitteth on the throne, and run from the wrath of the Lamb: For the great day of his wrath is come; and who shall be able to stand?' (Rev. 6: 12–17).

'And the seven angels came out of the temple, having the seven plagues, clothed in pure and white linen, and having their breasts girded with golden girdles. And one of the four beasts gave unto the seven angels seven golden vials full of the wrath of God, who liveth for ever and ever. And the temple was filled with smoke from the glory of God, and from his power; and no man was able to enter the temple, till the seven plagues of the seven angels were fulfilled' (Rev. 15: 6–8).

'And I heard a great voice out of the temple saying to the seven angels, Go your ways, and pour out the vials of the wrath of God upon the earth. And the first went, and poured out his vial upon the earth; and there fell a noisome and grievous sore upon the men which had the mark of the beast, and upon them which worshipped his image. And the second angel poured out his vial upon the sea; and it became as the blood of a dead man: and every living soul died in the sea. And the third angel poured out his vial upon the rivers and fountains of waters; and they became blood. And I heard the angel of the waters say, Thou art righteous, O Lord, which art, and wast, and shalt be, because thou hast judged thus. For they have shed the blood of saints and prophets, and thou hast given them blood to drink; for they are worthy. And I heard another out of the altar say, Even so, Lord God Almighty, true and righteous are thy judgments. And the fourth angel poured out his vial upon the sun; and power was given unto him to scorch men with fire. And the men were scorched with great heat, and blasphemed the name of God, which hath power over these plagues: and they repented not to give Him glory. And the fifth angel poured out his vial upon the seat of the beast; and his kingdom was full of darkness; and they gnawed their tongues for pain, and blasphemed the God of heaven because of their pains and their sores, and repented not of their deeds. And the sixth angel poured out his vial upon the great river Euphrates; and the water thereof was dried up, that the way of the kings of the east might be prepared. And I saw three unclean spirits like frogs come out of the mouth of the dragon, and out of the mouth of the beast, and out of the mouth of the false prophet. For they are the spirits of devils, working miracles, which go forth unto the kings of the earth and of the whole world, to gather them to the battle of that great day of God Almighty' (Rev. 16: 1–14). 'And he gathered them together into a place called in the Hebrew tongue ARMAGEDDON' (Rev. 16: 16).

'Then the seventh angel poured out his flask into the air; and a mighty shout came from the throne of the temple in heaven, saying, It is finished! Then the thunder crashed and rolled, and lightning flashed; and there was a great earthquake of a magnitude unprecedented in human history. The great city of "Babylon" split into three sections, and cities around the world fell in heaps of rubble; and so all

"Babylon's" sins were remembered in God's thoughts, and she was punished to the last drop of anger in the cup of the wine of the fierceness of His wrath. And islands vanished, and mountains flattened out, and there was an incredible hailstorm from heaven: hailstones weighing fifty kilogrammes fell from the sky on to the people below, and they cursed God because of the terrible hail' (Rev. 16: 17–21).

'And I saw heaven opened, and behold a white horse; and he that sat upon him was called Faithful and True, and in righteousness He doth judge and make war. His eyes were as a flame of fire, and on His head were many crowns; and he had a name written, that no man knew, but He himself. And he was clothed with a vesture dipped in blood: and his name is called the Word of God. And the armies which were in heaven followed him upon white horses, clothed in fine linen, white and clean. And out of his mouth goeth a sharp sword, that with it he should smite the nations: and he shall rule them with a rod of iron: and he treadeth the winepress of the fierceness and wrath of Almighty God. And he hath on his vesture and on His thigh a name written, KING OF KINGS, AND LORD OF LORDS. And I saw an angel standing in the sun; and he cried with a loud voice, saying to all the fowls that fly in the midst of heaven, Come and gather yourselves together unto the supper of the great God; that ye may eat the flesh of kings, and the flesh of captains, and the flesh of mighty men, and the flesh of horses, and of them that sit on them, and the flesh of all men, both free and bond, both small and great. And I saw the beast, and the kings of the earth, and their armies, gathered together to make war against him that sat on the horse, and against his army. And the beast was taken, and with him the false prophet that wrought miracles before him, with which he deceived them that had received the mark of the beast, and them that worshipped his image. These both were cast alive into a lake of fire burning with brimstone. And the remnant were slain with the sword of Him that sat upon the horse, which sword proceeded out of His mouth; and all the fowls were filled with their flesh' (Rev. 19: 11–21).

'And the seventh angel sounded; and there were great

voices in heaven, saying, The kingdoms of this world are become the kingdoms of our Lord, and of His Christ; and He shall reign for ever and ever' (Rev. 11: 15). 'But in the days of the voice of the seventh angel, when he shall begin to sound, the mystery of God should be finished, as He hath declared to his servants the prophets' (Rev. 10: 7).

## SATAN BOUND FOR 1000 YEARS

'Then I saw an angel come down from heaven with the key to the bottomless pit and a heavy chain in his hand. He seized the dragon – that old serpent, the devil, Satan – and bound him in chains for a thousand years, and threw him into the bottomless pit, which he then shut and locked, so that he could not fool the nations any more until the thousand years were finished. Afterwards he would be released again for a little while' (Rev. 20: 1–3).

## JUDGMENT OF AWARDS

'And he said, Go thy way, Daniel: for the words are closed up and sealed till the time of the end. Many shall be purified, and made white, and tried; but the wicked shall do wickedly: and none of the wicked shall understand; but the wise shall understand. And from the time that the daily sacrifice shall be taken away, and the abomination that maketh desolate set up, there shall be a thousand two hundred and ninety days. Blessed is he that waiteth and cometh to the thousand three hundred and five and thirty days. But go thou thy way till the end be: for thou shalt rest, and stand in thy lot at the end of the days' (Dan. 12: 9–13).

*After the battle of Armageddon there will be forty-five days in which the Judgment Seat of Christ is set* (Rev. 11: 18). *All believers, including the Old Testament saints, will appear before the Lord to receive the awards for things done in the earthly body. Blessed are they that remain until the 1,335th day. These are the 144,000 from the twelve Tribes of Israel, who were sealed on earth, before the Wrath of God, and all those who were left of the nations who came against Jerusalem. They shall go up from year to year, to worship the King of Kings, the Lord of Hosts, and to keep the Feast of Tabernacles* (Zech. 14: 16 LB). *The 1,335th day sets the start of the Millennium Reign.*

'And the seventh angel sounded; and there were great voices in heaven, saying, The kingdoms of this world are become the kingdoms of our Lord, and of his Christ; and he shall reign for ever and ever. And the four and twenty elders which sat before God on their seats fell upon their faces, and worshipped God, saying, We give thee thanks, O Lord God Almighty, which art, and wast, and art to come; because thou hast taken to thee thy great power and hast reigned. And the nations were angry, and thy wrath is come, and the time of the dead, that they should be judged, and that thou shouldest give reward unto thy servants the prophets, and to the saints, and them that fear thy name, small and great; and shouldest destroy them which destroy the earth. And the temple of God was opened in heaven, and there was seen in His temple the ark of His testament: and there were lightnings, and voices, and thunderings, and an earthquake and great hail' (Rev. 11: 15–19).

*The Judgment Seat of Christ is not a judgment of believers' sins but of their works. For those who have been born again, the precious blood of Jesus has cleansed them of all unrighteousness; their sins are not only forgiven, but also blotted out. Salvation is a free gift of God through Jesus Christ.*

'For by grace are ye saved through faith; and that not of yourselves: it is the gift of God: not of works, lest any man should boast.' (Eph. 2: 8–9). 'He that heareth my word and believeth on Him that sent me, hath everlasting life, and shall not come into condemnation, but is passed from death unto life (John 5: 24). 'And their sins and iniquities will I remember no more' (Heb. 10: 17). 'None of his sins that he hath committed shall be mentioned unto him; he hath done that which is lawful and right; he shall surely live' (Ezek. 33: 16). 'Every man's work shall be made manifest, for the day shall declare it, because it shall be revealed by fire, and the fire shall try every man's work of what sort it is. If any man's work abide which he hath built thereupon, he shall receive a reward. If any man's work whall be burned, he shall suffer loss, but he himself shall be saved yet so as by fire' (1 Cor. 3: 13–15).

*There will be special rewards in heaven for those who are persecuted for righteousness' sake.*

'Blessed are they which are persecuted for righteousness' sake: for theirs is the kingdom of heaven. Blessed are ye, when men shall revile you, and persecute you, and shall say all manner of evil against you falsely, for my sake. Rejoice, and be exceeding glad: for great is your reward in heaven: for so persecuted they the prophets which were before you' (Matt. 5: 10–12). 'And Jesus said unto them, Verily I say unto you, That ye which have followed me, in the regeneration when the Son of man shall sit in the throne of His glory, ye also shall sit upon twelve thrones, judging the twelve tribes of Israel' (Matt. 19: 28).

*This position of authority is given not only to the Apostles, but will be awarded also to all those who overcame.*

'And he that overcometh, and keepeth my works unto the end, to him will I give power over the nations: and he shall rule them with a rod of iron; as the vessels of a potter shall they be broken to shivers: . . .' (Rev. 2: 26–7).

*Jesus also tells us that all those who will be killed, rather than take the mark of the beast, will live and reign with Him for a thousand years. At the Judgment Seat of Christ, the saints will be assigned their positions in the Kingdom, and be given their place of authority and rulership over the nations during the next one thousand years of the Millennium Reign.*

'Do ye not know that the saints shall judge the world? . . . Know ye not that we shall judge angels?' (1 Cor. 6: 2–3).

# THE MILLENNIUM – THE LORD JESUS RETURNS TO THE EARTH AND REIGNS FOR A THOUSAND YEARS

*At the battle of Armageddon, Christ will return to the earth in great glory, followed by all the armies of heaven, the saints who are now clothed in their immortal bodies and wearing the white robes of righteousness* (Rev. 19: 11–14). *The Lord will crush the power of the Antichrist and destroy the armies of the world which have gathered against Jerusalem, casting the Beast and the False Prophet into the lake of fire for ever, and binding Satan in the bottomless pit for a thousand years. When He stands upon the Mount of Olives to execute this judgment, the mountain shall split in two, creating a huge valley into which the 144,000 Jews who have been sealed with the mark of God will escape from the terrible destruction. The Lord Jesus will then reign upon the earth with the saints for a thousand years, and under His rule the world will flourish in perfect peace and prosperity.*

'Behold the day of the Lord cometh, and thy spoil shall be divided in the midst of thee. For I will gather all nations against Jerusalem to battle; and the city shall be taken, and the houses rifled, and the women ravished; and half the city shall go forth into captivity, and the residue of the people shall not be cut off from the city. Then shall the Lord go forth, and fight against those nations, as when he fought in the day of battle.

'And His feet shall stand in that day upon the mount of Olives, which is before Jerusalem on the east, and the mount of Olives shall cleave in the midst thereof toward the east and toward the west, and there shall be a very great valley; and half of the mountain shall remove toward the north and half of it toward the south. And ye shall flee to the valley of the mountains... and the LORD my God shall come and all the saints with thee...

'And the LORD shall be king over all the earth: in that day there shall be one LORD, and His name one. All the land shall be turned as a plain... And men shall dwell in it, and there shall be no more utter destruction; but Jerusalem shall be safely inhabited' (Zech. 14: 1–11).

*On that day, the Jews will recognise Jesus as their Messiah:* 'They will look on Him they pierced' (Zech. 12: 10 LB), *and repent and mourn because of their sins in rejecting Him. The Lord will pour out the spirit of grace and prayer on the people of Jerusalem. All the families that remain will weep in profound sorrow; the entire nation will be bowed down in universal grief. Then Jesus will be worshipped in the place where He was rejected. Israel will understand that Jesus was wounded and bruised for our sins. He was chatised that we might have peace, and by His wounds we are healed. At last the Jews will acknowledge Jesus as their Lord and Saviour. Righteousness shall cover the earth and perfect peace shall reign throughout the world.*

'No longer will babies die when only a few days old; no longer will men be considered old at 100! Only sinners will die that young! In those days, when a man builds a house, he will keep on living in it – it will not be destroyed by invading armies as in the past. My people will plant vineyards and eat the fruit themselves – their enemies will not confiscate it. For my people will live as long as trees and will enjoy their hard-won gains. Their harvests will not be eaten by their enemies; their children will not be born to be cannon fodder. For they are the children of those the Lord has blessed; and their children, too, shall be blessed. I will answer them before they even call to me. While they are still talking to me about their needs, I will go ahead and answer their prayers' (Isa. 65: 20–4 LB).

'In that day the wolf and the lamb will lie down together, and the leopard and goats will be at peace. Calves and fat cattle will be safe among lions, and a little child shall lead them all. The cows will graze among bears; cubs and calves will lie down together, and lions will eat grass like the cows. Babies will crawl safely among poisonous snakes, and a little child who puts his hand in a nest of deadly adders will pull it out unharmed. Nothing will hurt or destroy in all my holy mountain, for as the waters fill the sea, so shall the earth be full of the knowledge of the Lord' (Isa. 11: 6–9 LB).

*God's promise to Abraham will be fulfilled: the Jews will live in peace and safety in their own land, which never again shall be taken from them; the land which God promised Abraham and his seed for ever.*

'And in that day thou [the Jews] shalt say, O Lord, I will praise thee: though thou wast angry with me, thine anger is turned away, and thou comfortedst me. Behold, God is my salvation; I will trust, and not be afraid: for the Lord JEHOVAH is my strength and my song; he also is become my salvation. Therefore with joy shall we draw water out of the wells of salvation. And in that day shall ye say, Praise the Lord, call upon his name, declare his doings among the people, make mention that his name is exalted. Sing unto the Lord; for he hath done excellent things: this is known in all the earth. Cry out and shout, thou inhabitant of Zion: for great is the Holy One of Israel in the midst of thee' (Isa. 12).

'And it shall come to pass that everyone that is left of all the nations which came against Jerusalem shall even go up from year to year to worship the King, the Lord of hosts, and to keep the feast of tabernacles. And it shall be, that whoso will not come up of all the families of the earth unto Jerusalem to worship the King, the Lord of hosts, even upon them shall be no rain. And if the family of Egypt go not up and come not, [they shall have no rain: the Lord shall plague the heathens' land with drought who] come not up to keep the feast of tabernacles. This shall be the punishment of Egypt, and the punishment of all nations that come not up to keep the feast of tabernacles' (Zech. 14: 16–19).

*Although the earth will enjoy a thousand years of peace, it is still not the perfect age; there will still be those who will rebel against God's laws. All free moral agents must be tested; there must be no time, in the ages to come, for another rebellion to break out. It is a terrible fact, but true, that when men are permitted the divine gift of free will, there will be those who will deliberately pursue the way of self-will. There will be those who choose to rebel against the Lord's call to attend the Feast of Tabernacles each year. As a result the rain will be withheld from their lands. In their hearts they will resent God's discipline, though they will not be able to*

186

*disrupt the order and harmony of Christ's reign on earth.*

*At the end of the thousand years, Satan will be let out of his prison for the last time to test the inhabitants of the earth, and to lead the rebellious children on a march against Jerusalem:*

'Satan shall be loosed out of his prison, and shall go out to deceive the nations which are in the four quarters of the earth, Gog and Magog, to gather them together to battle: the number of whom is as the sand of the sea. And they went up on the breadth of the earth, and compassed the camp of the saints about, and the beloved city: and fire came down from God out of heaven, and devoured them' (Rev. 20: 7–9).

*Satan's time for eternal banishment has come.*

'And the devil that deceived them was cast into the lake of fire and brimstone, where the beast and the false prophet are, and shall be tormented day and night for ever' (Rev. 20: 10).

## GREAT WHITE THRONE JUDGMENT

'Marvel not at this: for the hour is coming, in the which all that are in the graves shall hear his voice, and shall come forth; they that have done good, unto the resurrection of life; and they that have done evil, unto the resurrection of damnation' (John 5: 28–9).

'But now is Christ risen from the dead, and become the firstfruits of them that slept. For since by man came death, by man came also the resurrection of the dead. For as in Adam all die, even so in Christ shall all be made alive. But every man in his own order: Christ the firstfruits; afterward they that are Christ's at His coming. Then cometh the end, when He shall have delivered up the kingdom to God, even the Father; when He shall have put down all rule and all authority and power. For He must reign till he hath put all enemies under His feet. The last enemy that shall be destroyed is death' (1 Cor. 15: 20–6).

*Christ, at His resurrection, was the 'firstfruits of them that slept'. The firstfruits consisted of the first and finest sheaf of the harvest given to the priest to be offered as a sacrifice to God. Jesus was the chief ear of wheat in that sheaf which contained other prime ears of wheat. These are the saints who rose from the graves when Jesus broke their captivity in Hades and rose from the dead.*

'And the graves were opened; and many bodies of the saints which slept arose, and came out of the graves after his resurrection, and went into the holy city and appeared unto many' (Matt. 27: 52-3).

*In the book of Revelation, we see this company of firstfruits before the throne of God, singing a song that none but they could learn.*

'These are they which were not defiled with women; for they are virgins. These are they which followeth the Lamb withersoever He goeth. These were redeemed from among men, being the firstfruits unto God and to the Lamb. And in their mouth was found no guile: for they are without fault before the throne of God' (Rev. 14: 4-5).

*We see that this company of firstfruits is before the throne of God during the time that the Antichrist is making war on the saints on earth. These are followed by 'them that are Christ's at His coming', the Bride of Christ caught out of the world at the Rapture.*

'For the Lord Himself shall descend from heaven with a shout, with the voice of the archangel, and with the trump of God: and the dead in Christ shall rise first: then we which are alive and remain shall be caught up together with them in the clouds to meet the Lord in the air: and so shall we ever be with the Lord' (1 Thess. 4: 16-17). 'But the rest of the dead lived not again until the thousand years were finished' (Rev. 20: 5).

*The first resurrection has been at the time of Christ's Second Coming, the Rapture. This second resurrection, occurring at the end of the thousand years' reign of peace is a resurrection of all the unjust, the unbelievers, that have ever lived, and those righteous people who have lived during the millennium: Regardless of when or where death terminated man's earthly existence, God is able to raise him from the dead to stand before the Great White Throne.*

'And I saw a great white throne, and him that sat on it, from whose face the earth and the heaven fled away; and there was found no place for them. And I saw the dead, small and great, stand before God; and the books were opened: and another book was opened, which is the book of life: and the dead were judged out of those things which were written in the books, according to their works. And the sea gave up the dead which were in it; and death and hell delivered up the dead which were in them, and they were judged every man according to their works. And death and hell were cast into the lake of fire. This is the second death. And whosoever was not found written in the book of life was cast into the lake of fire' (Rev. 20: 11–15).

*The Book of Life will be opened, and all the righteous people who have lived and died during the thousand years of peace, and whose names are found written in the Book, will be raised to everlasting life. But for the unbeliever whose name is not there, what a terrible thing it will be to stand before that Great White Throne.*

'But I say unto you, That every idle word that men shall speak, they shall give account thereof in the day of judgment. For by thy words thou shalt be justified, and by thy words thou shalt be condemned' (Matt. 12: 36–7).

*The recording of the person's life will be played back, and in that dreadful moment he will hear past conversations, cursing, evil words of contempt, the refusal to accept Jesus. Everything is on record; the sinner's own words will condemn him.*

'For nothing is secret, that shall not be made manifest; neither anything hid, that shall not be known and come abroad' (Luke 8: 17).

*His sentence will be announced – 'Depart from me.' THE WAGES OF SIN IS DEATH. Every knee shall bow and every tongue confess that Jesus Christ is Lord. Before the sinner departs, to face the second death, the lake of fire, he must bow the knee and confess that Jesus Christ is Lord. Once the judgment of the wicked dead is over, Death and Hell will be cast into the lake of fire. Victory over the last enemy, Death, will then be complete. God at this time will burn up the earth and provide a perfect new world.*

'The Lord is not slack concerning his promise, as some men count slackness; but is long-suffering to us-ward, not willing that any should perish, but that all should come to repentance. But the day of the Lord will come as a thief in the night; in the which the heavens shall pass away with a great noise, and the elements shall melt with fervent heat, the earth also and the works that are therein shall be burned up. Seeing then that all these things shall be dissolved, what manner of persons ought ye to be in all holy conversation and godliness. Looking for and hasting unto the coming of the day of God, wherein the heavens being on fire shall be dissolved, and the elements shall melt with fervent heat? Nevertheless we, according to his promise, look for new heavens and a new earth, wherein dwelleth reighteousness' (2 Pet. 3: 9–13).

## A NEW HEAVEN AND A NEW EARTH

*The former things will then be passed away and shall be remembered no more: the past will be blotted out. The new heaven and the new earth usher in perfect eternity. The earth will again become the garden of Eden. In that wonderful, wonderful day, God Himself will dwell with us: the fellowship that the Lord had with man in the garden of Eden will be fully restored. Hallelujah! The gift of God is eternal life through Jesus Christ our Saviour.*

'And I saw a new heaven and a new earth: for the first heaven and the first earth were passed away; and there was no more sea. And I, John, saw the holy city, new Jerusalem, coming down from God out of heaven, prepared as a bride adorned for her husband. And I heard a great voice out of heaven saying, Behold, the tabernacle of God is with men, and He will dwell with them, and they shall be His people, and God Himself shall be with them, and be their God. And God shall wipe away all tears from their eyes; and there shall be no more death, neither sorrow, nor crying, neither shall there be any more pain: for the former things are passed away' (Rev. 21: 1–4).

*There shall be nothing there which is evil, for the Throne of God and the Lamb will be there, and His servants will worship Him. They shall see His face, and His name shall be written in their foreheads; there will be no night and no need for lamps or the sun, for the Lord God will be their light, and they shall reign for ever and ever.*

'Then the angel said to me: these words are trustworthy and true. I am coming soon. God, who tells His prophets what the future holds, has sent His angel to tell you . . . THIS WILL HAPPEN SOON! (Rev. 22: 6–7 LB).

## A SINNER'S PRAYER

*My heavenly Father, I come to you in the name of Jesus. Lord, I recognise that I am a sinner, and I ask you today to forgive me of all my sins, and to cleanse me from all unrighteousness. I believe that Jesus Christ is the Son of God, and that Jesus rose from the dead, and sits at your right hand. Thank you Lord Jesus for dying on the Cross for me. Thank you Lord Jesus for forgiving me of my sins. Please fill me with your Holy Spirit, and write my name in the Lamb's Book of Life. Amen.*